POLICING IN MILWAUKEE
A STRATEGIC HISTORY

George L. Kelling

POLICING IN MILWAUKEE

A STRATEGIC HISTORY

MARQUETTE
UNIVERSITY
PRESS

URBAN LIFE SERIES
No. 8
THOMAS J. JABLONSKY, SERIES EDITOR

© 2015 Marquette University Press
Milwaukee, Wisconsin 53201-3141
All rights reserved.
www.marquette.edu/mupress/

LIBRARY OF CONGRESS CATALOGUING-IN-PUBLICATION DATA

Kelling, George L.
Policing in Milwaukee : a strategic history / by George L. Kelling.
   pages cm. — (Urban life series ; No. 8)
Includes bibliographical references and index.
ISBN 978-1-62600-300-2 (pbk. : alk. paper) — ISBN 1-62600-
300-9 (pbk. : alk. paper)
1. Police—Wisconsin—Milwaukee—History. 2. Police administra-
tion—Wisconsin—Milwaukee—History. 3. Community policing—
Wisconsin—Milwaukee—History. 4. Police-community relations—
Wisconsin—Milwaukee—History. I. Title.
HV8148.M498K45 2015
363.209775'95—dc23
                                         2015020771

∞The paper used in this publication meets the minimum requirements of the
American National Standard for Information Sciences—
Permanence of Paper for Printed Library Materials, ANSI Z39.48-1992.

MARQUETTE UNIVERSITY PRESS
MILWAUKEE

The Association of Jesuit University Presses

CONTENTS

PREFACE

This is a book about policing in Milwaukee. Although primarily an analytical and historical account, it is motivated nevertheless by three elements from my own life experiences. First, my personal past as a native of Milwaukee and resident of the local community for twenty-five years as well as ongoing family ties there have left me with an enduring commitment to my hometown and interest in understanding its historical evolution. Second, throughout my forty-five year professional career as a researcher and scholar in American policing and as a consultant to police organizations throughout the country and internationally, policing activities in Milwaukee frequently drew my attention—at times for their excellence, at other times because of the need for change. Finally, over the last few decades I have had opportunities to work on a professional basis directly with the Milwaukee Police Department (hereafter, MPD) as well as other groups and agencies linked with the criminal justice system in the city. Most recently this involved consulting work with the MPD just prior to and during the administration of the current chief, Edward Flynn, who took office in 2008.

Reflecting these different perspectives, the narrative that follows represents a culmination of both personal and professional interests with Milwaukee at the core. Accordingly, before turning explicitly to the examination of the MPD within the context of American policing that makes up the remainder of this volume, I pause here to reflect briefly upon a few pertinent experiences that shaped my personal impressions of Milwaukee's history and my later professional development. I also describe various professional contacts I have had with the MPD and other local criminal justice agencies. In my mind, all have contributed to my formulation of the discussion that follows... perhaps none so strongly as my earliest memories of Milwaukee as a youth.

MILWAUKEE: A PERSONAL PAST

The world was very different when I was a boy in Milwaukee during the 1940s. It was not necessarily a better world—with the Great Depression, a world war, Jim Crow as the law of the American South and de facto segregation as the law of the North, and the birth of the nuclear age. But in at least one respect it was better: I grew up in a world in which neither my parents nor I felt threatened by crime.

My earliest recollections are of living on 27th Street, in Milwaukee's Seventh Ward. Reflecting the traditions of a mixed-use, German neighborhood it took a short walk of only a couple blocks to reach a neighborhood tavern, butcher shop, drug store, and bakery. When I was still very young my family moved to 47th Street on the northwest side, an area more residential where I spent most of my childhood (ages six to fifteen). Our house lay directly across from Parklawn, one of the first public housing developments in the United States: a low-rise development constructed in 1936/37 as part of the federal government's slum clearance and low-rent program administered by the Public Works Administration. Political fears that it would house African Americans led to the city's decision to site Parklawn in a semirural area at Milwaukee's urban edge. It covered eight square blocks, comprised of 518 townhouse and apartment units arranged in eight residential "courts" with a large U-shaped park and playground. Only six units were actually allocated to African Americans.[1] If there was any stigma attached to living in or near Parklawn, it escaped me: certainly low-income families made their homes there, but this was the era of the Depression and World War Two and many, if not most, families were considered working class.

For me as a youngster, the neighborhood was great, with a lot of kids, a park, playground, a creek, woods, and an old soccer field a few blocks away that could be used for hardball. I recall long summer days with friends—most from Parklawn—that began early and lasted until dark each night. During the school year I walked to school, came home for lunch, and after school and dinner was out sledding, ice skating, or hanging out with friends until dark: our parents had little concern for our safety so we were largely left free to roam. My parents warned me against hitchhiking (which I did anyway), and accepting

---

1   Julie Boatright Wilson, "Milwaukee: Industrial Metropolis on the Lake" (unpublished monograph, Harvard University, April 1955), 61.

money or rides from strangers, especially when I went to the downtown arcade to play games. Public transportation was safe and drivers
carried change and sold passes; houses had "milk chutes"—openings
with small doors near back entrances where deliveries could be left; bi-
cycles were parked unlocked in backyards. Security in my high school
consisted of an honor student at a desk at the main entrance.

After graduating from Washington High School in 1952 and going
off to attend college at St. Olaf in Minnesota, I returned to Milwaukee
during the summers of 1953 and 1954 to work on a playground at
Siefert Elementary School along 14th Street in the inner city. During
the first year, the playground was mixed racially—not integrated because whites hung with whites and blacks with blacks, and teams in the
evening softball league were either all white or all black. Nonetheless
the playground was peaceful, with only one incident occurring when
a brawl started during a game. It was not clear to me whether the
brawl was racially motivated or a matter of two teams fighting it out.
Nevertheless, once the teams were separated blacks were on one side
of the playground and whites on the other. Fortunately, the night ended uneventfully and there were no consequences in the days that followed. When I was asked to return to Siefert during the next summer,
the world was very different: the playground was now all black. The
coaches (who were white) became intimidated by kids on the playground and regularly called police to maintain control. I never called
police, although an amiable foot officer did stop by regularly to say
hello, no doubt checking things out.

For the most part, well into the 1950s then, my family and I moved
around freely and still felt safe in these neighborhoods of my youth.
This relatively benign world ended during the 1960s when crime, the
fear of crime, and urban disorder exploded in Milwaukee and so many
other cities across the country. And also by the 1960s I was finding my
way into events and institutions at the center of the tumult, developing increasing interests in issues of social welfare and social justice, and
beginning a professional career in criminal justice itself.

POLICING:
A PROFESSIONAL LIFE BEGUN IN MILWAUKEE

My entry into criminal justice was in many senses as directly linked
to Milwaukee as was my youth. Soon after attending St. Olaf College,

I worked in a juvenile detention center and as a probation officer in Minneapolis. Returning to Milwaukee in 1960, after completing a Master's Degree in Social Work at the University of Wisconsin-Milwaukee (UWM), I became Assistant Superintendent of Juvenile Detention for Milwaukee County. I left Milwaukee for two years to oversee childcare and social work at a children's psychiatric facility in Minnesota, but returned in 1965 to teach courses in corrections at UWM's School of Social Work.

It was while teaching at UWM during the 1960s that I first became interested in policing. Police were highly visible and controversial during this period, the era of civil rights and anti-war protests; furthermore, my teaching specialty derived directly from my experience in crime control and corrections. While on the faculty at UWM I met and began working with the Commandos, a militant civil rights group in the city. I also began serving as a consultant to the Milwaukee police union which put me into regular contact with police. This contact developed into a relationship with the union that would continue for several decades. I recount these experiences with the Commandos and the police union in greater detail in the chapters that follow as they pertain specifically to events and changes involving the MPD. Finally, collaborating with several local police officials (none from the MPD), I wrote the grant that started what would ultimately become the Department of Criminal Justice at UWM.

In 1970 I moved to UW-Madison to do my Ph.D. and have not lived in Milwaukee since. During this time I have worked as a researcher in policing, an academic, and a consultant: first, heading major research projects at the Police Foundation in Washington, D.C., and in the Program in Criminal Justice Policy and Management at Harvard University's John F. Kennedy School of Government; then teaching criminal justice (while continuing research) at Northeastern University and Rutgers University. My two most noteworthy research projects are the *Kansas City Preventive Patrol Experiment* (1975) and the *Newark Foot Patrol Experiment* (1981), both funded by the Police Foundation.[2] Moreover, over the years I have worked as a consultant for many troubled police departments, most notably New York City in

2   The Ford Foundation created the Police Foundation with a thirty million dollar endowment in 1970 to improve policing. Since then, many communities have created local police foundations. George L. Kelling et al., *The Kansas City Preventive Patrol Experiment* (Washinton, D.C.: Police

the 1980s and 1990s, Los Angeles during the early twenty-first century, Detroit in 2012-13, and currently in New York City again.

A central thread in my research, consulting, and writing throughout this time has been a focus on "going to the ground," seeking to understand actual happenings as they take place and how they hold meaning for citizens themselves, as well as police, within a local context. The origins of this thread lay in my Milwaukee experiences, from working on playgrounds during college to learning the ropes as a criminal justice practitioner and not merely scholar. They also derive from the mentoring of Professor of Anthropology Edward Wellin, a teaching colleague at the UWM in the 1960s who continually emphasized how important it was for researchers to have first-hand, grass-roots experience. I never forgot this lesson which has shaped my research and analytical work powerfully. I have discovered that police organizations look very different from the top down and bottom up; that crime problems and data often are mischaracterized without meticulous direct observation; and that crime prevention and reduction efforts may be most effective when aimed at small concrete changes on the ground. Above all, small things matter a lot. Data collection in my projects typically has included riding, bicycling, and walking with police officers on their beats; meeting with citizens on streets, in their homes, and places of worship; conducting direct observations on my own; and simply talking with ordinary people (not only residents but shop owners, pastors, health and service providers, and others with vested interests in neighborhoods) about their perceptions of their own neighborhoods, events, and problems.

The analyses and conclusions that I have written about in research reports and publications reflect these elements, as do my attempts to guide police practice in consulting even today. The findings presented in the "Broken Windows" article I co-authored with the late James Q. Wilson, published in the *Atlantic* in 1982, came from walking with beat cops in Newark and meeting with citizens who wanted to talk about what they saw as the most urgent problems in their local neighborhoods in Boston, Newark, and many other cities.[3] In the article we proposed that small, seemingly insignificant things that bother

Foundation, 1975); George L. Kelling et al., *The Newark Foot Patrol Experiment* (Washington, D.C.: Police Foundation, 1981).

3   James Q. Wilson and George L. Kelling, "The Police and Neighborhood Safety," *The Atlantic* (March 1982): 29-38.

citizens in neighborhoods—graffiti, trash, street prostitution, loud noises, small-scale drug dealing in parks—actually might be very significant for police to address, not only because they represent citizen concerns and priorities, but because they may also be precursors to an influx of other violent and predatory crimes.

Similarly, *Fixing Broken Windows*, which I wrote with my anthropologist/lawyer wife Catherine Coles, recounts the turnaround of the New York City subway system, where everyone was certain—when I began work there—that the main problem underlying crime was homelessness.[4] The assumption that followed was that nothing could be done about crime unless the precipitating causes of homelessness were eliminated—leaving police in a hopeless, impotent role. Only after careful, detailed observations of events and activities in the subway did it become clear to me that homeless people were not themselves the cause of increased crime. Instead, the problem was particular illegal behaviors such as aggressive panhandling, dangerous blocking of passageways and platforms, and farebeating. An appropriate intervention and crime reduction program had to be formulated that targeted these activities—not the homeless. It was no surprise to me that crime fell dramatically once police and their community partners began to address the real problems which were discovered through careful study of activities on the ground.

I owe a great debt then to Milwaukee, both as the locus for a personal past that has served me well and as a context that provided rich ground for professional growth extending to a wider stage. As I have progressed through the years in developing a deeper and more extensive understanding of American policing—its history, changes in the basic definition of the profession held by police themselves, the evolution of particular strategies and tactics used by police, successes and failures of police as they have sought to adapt to societal and cultural changes—Milwaukee has remained at the forefront of my interests. At various times I have been closer to police matters and crime issues there than at others, in part due to contacts with family members and friends living in Milwaukee neighborhoods, with police union officials, with the Bradley Foundation (which contributed funding toward the publication of *Fixing Broken Windows*), and with academic colleagues

---

4   See George L. Kelling and Catherine M. Coles, *Fixing Broken Windows: Restoring Order and Reducing Crime in Our Communities* (New York: The Free Press, 1996).

located in Wisconsin who shared my interests. The account that follows represents the culmination of my ongoing professional commitment to a place that remains both dear to me and intensely interesting.

ACKNOWLEDGMENTS

I thank Janet Riordan (Director of Community Programs), the staff, and board of the Lynde and Harry Bradley Foundation for their financial and moral support of this book. I wrote it without pressure, either in terms of time or substance, from the Foundation. Chief Edward Flynn provided me with complete access to the Milwaukee Police Department, a privilege that I deeply appreciate. Assistant Chief James Harpole was unbelievably helpful, both as a source himself and as a person knowledgeable about where to look if he did not have direct access to particular material. Deputy Chief John Hagen (Ret.) was also a goldmine of information and documents. Likewise, Chief of Staff Joel Plant went out of his way to accommodate my requests and review contemporary material to assure its accuracy. Inspector Steven Basting provided and trusted me with temporary possession of historical materials, including departmental reports that date back to the 1930s. Anne Schwartz, formerly the MPD's Public Relations Manager and former reporter that she was, provided me with a wealth of background information about the MPD and its political environment. Heidi Henricks, Senior Staff Assistant to the Chief of Police, patiently got me to the right person when I couldn't figure who I should talk to or how should I go about finding that person.

Of course many other persons provided me with assistance in a variety of ways: referring me to sources, being interviewed, providing data and, at times, reviewing some of my written materials to be certain they were accurate. I appreciate their help. Special thanks to Thomas J. Jablonsky, this series editor, for his thoughtful editorial and substantive contributions to this book. Finally, I thank my wife, Catherine M. Coles, who in editing this book tolerated my ellipses, passive voice, disorder, and other grammatical failings. She was incredibly helpful, not just providing editing but in sharpening my thinking and presentation.

INTRODUCTION

The analytical framework presented in the chapters that follow is grounded in my understanding and analyses of strategic developments in American policing that took place from the middle decades of the twentieth century into the first decade of the next.[1] This span of roughly fifty years began with the MPD a prestigious leader in policing, recognized nationally and internationally. Within a short twenty years, however, the department had become isolated within the local Milwaukee community and fallen well behind the leading edge of policing in the United States. Moving into the twenty-first century the MPD began to show clear signs of reversing its previous decline and resuming its once dominant position as a leader in American policing.

This book addresses the questions of how and why these dramatic transformations have taken place. While the central purpose is to examine and document MPD attempts at confronting and crafting responses to changes taking place within the local community, the department also has been influenced by national policing practices and crime problems. In this regard my account may be viewed as a case study in the history of American policing, for the experiences of the MPD reflect those of police organizations around the country and parallel changes within the whole of American policing as a professional field.

This Introduction provides an overview of some of the historical antecedents of contemporary American policing that shaped Milwaukee's experience as well. These include a heritage that began with Anglo Saxon policing in England; the nineteenth century period when American policing was dominated primarily by local political interests; the Reform Era, with its countervailing influences against

---

1 George L. Kelling and Mark H. Moore, *The Evolving Strategy of Policing*, Perspectives on Policing 4 (National Institute of Justice, U.S. Department of Justice, and the Program in Criminal Justice Policy and Management, John F. Kennedy School of Government, Harvard University, November 1988).

corruption and cronyism, covering the late nineteenth century up to the middle of the twentieth century; and finally an age of community policing that began slowly during the 1980s and continues to develop and mature today.

ANGLO-SAXON ROOTS OF AMERICAN POLICING

At their best, as do all American police, Milwaukee's police stand in the Anglo Saxon tradition. Sir Robert Peel, the English Prime Minister considered the father of modern Anglo Saxon policing, articulated this tradition in 1829 when creating London's Metropolitan Police— Scotland Yard. The principles of policing he espoused harkened back to the medieval tithing system in which families were obligated to prevent crime and apprehend offenders and yet they also looked to the future, anticipating the emergence of organizational policing in urban industrial centers. Obligating families may have been feasible in rural agrarian society where everybody knew each other in a community, but it failed in the context of anonymity within emerging industrial centers. Peel would introduce a new policing model: the basic mission was to prevent crime and disorder; police ability to carry out their mission would depend on public support; and physical force should be used only when persuasion failed. Detective work (criminal investigation) remained in the private sector, at least initially. The mission and its underlying rationale were captured in Peel's most famous principle:

> Police, at all times, should maintain a relationship with the public that gives reality to the historic tradition that the police are the public and the public are the police; the police being the only members of the public who are paid to give full-time attention to duties which are incumbent upon every citizen in the interests of community welfare and existence.[2]

To be sure, no American police department has fully lived up to these principles; nevertheless they remain a standard against which police, citizens and political leaders can take stock of police organizations and activities. Moreover, embedded in them is a more basic belief: if we assume that citizens possess the right to govern themselves, it follows that they also have the right to police themselves. Although citizens in a complex society delegate authority for this function to

---

2   W. L. Melville Lee, *A History of Police in England* (London: Methuen, 1901), Chap. 12.

surrogates—that is, police dedicated to ensuring public safety and paid for their services—the obligation of "self policing" on the part of citizens remains.

In operational terms the core of Anglo Saxon policing was comprised of conspicuous officers (thus avoiding secret police as they were used at the time in French continental policing) embedded in small geographical areas or beats who patrolled their areas on foot. The purpose of patrolling was to prevent crime through police presence, reducing opportunities for crime and maintaining order. These basic tactics began in England and spread to the United States where police employed them in urban centers until well into the twentieth century.[3] The fundamental notion of preventive patrol in neighborhoods continues to be the central operational approach of modern American policing today—if not in actual practice, rhetorically as "the backbone of policing."

THE NINETEENTH CENTURY POLITICAL ERA IN AMERICAN POLICING

Police departments that developed during the young United States from the eighteenth and into the nineteenth centuries were both similar to and different from their English models. They were similar in that police adopted the same practices of patrolling particular beats for the purposes of preventing crime. Detective work slowly moved into both English and American policing during the late nineteenth and early twentieth centuries, although it retained a lowly status until the 1920s and 1930s in part because of the corruption that often accompanied it.[4] American urban police during the nineteenth century were different from English police, however, in that they were products of the urban political structure prevalent in the United States at the

---

3   Wilber R. Miller, *Cops and Bobbies: Police Authority in New York and London* (Chicago: University of Chicago Press, 1973).

4   See Anthony A. Braga, Edward A. Flynn, George L. Kelling, and Christine M. Cole, *Moving the Work of Criminal Investigators Towards Crime Control*, New Perspectives in Policing (National Institute of Justice, U.S. Department of Justice, and John F. Kennedy School of Government, Harvard University, March, 2011), for a brief history of criminal investigation.

time.[5] In respects, during the nineteenth century cities in this country were collections of tribes: as the original English and Dutch settlers gave way to immigrants from Eastern Europe, distinctive groups tended to cluster in areas of cities commonly called wards. Although joined together within cities, these wards were semi-autonomous political units headed by elected councilmen or, as they came to be called, "ward bosses." Ward bosses largely controlled how services were dispensed in their wards and who was hired to disburse them—in other words cities were run through a local patronage system.

Police were overlaid on this patronage system with police precincts superimposed on political wards. Although citywide in name and headed by a chief, each police department was administered effectively at the ward or precinct level. Ward bosses appointed police captains who ran the precincts; in turn, the precinct captain appointed local police officers. If a new ward boss was elected it was likely that a fresh captain would appoint a different set of police officers. Police were usually of the same ethnic group as local residents and related to families who lived there. Operationally, in this political world police were the primary providers of social and governmental services: police stations offered housing for newly arrived immigrants, and police ran the original soup and bread lines. They regularly checked local stores and shops to make sure they were properly secured at night. Social control was often exercised informally rather than carried out through the use of criminal justice procedures, with officers on the beat resolving conflicts and neighborhood disputes on a routine basis.[6]

For all the good they did during the nineteenth century, police essentially became "adjuncts" to often corrupt political machines, as historian Robert Fogelson has written.[7] The entire system ultimately gave rise to police corruption, particularly political corruption as police worked to protect their jobs by helping to ensure that ward bosses were reelected. Milwaukee was no exception to this pattern. But

---

5   There is a substantial literature on this period. See for example, Samuel Walker, *A Critical History of Police Reform* (Lexington, MA: Lexington Books, 1977).

6   Eric H. Monkkonen, *Police in Urban America: 1860-1920* (Cambridge: Cambridge University Press, 1981).

7   Robert Fogelson, *Big City Police* (Cambridge: Harvard University Press, 1977), 37.

Milwaukee also became a leader, if not *the* leader, in the national move to reform nineteenth century urban policing that followed.

THE MID-TWENTIETH CENTURY REFORM ERA IN AMERICAN POLICING

During the twentieth century, policing in the United States followed a course that ultimately departed from the most basic principles and goals of its Anglo Saxon heritage. The motivation for these changes actually arose, however, from the perceived need to rein in and eliminate the pervasive corruption and political control over police by local officials. This new Reform Era paradigm in policing sought to professionalize police, giving them greater autonomy and protecting them from political influence: it brought tenure for chiefs; accorded police civil service status which meant they could be fired only for cause and not at will; and lodged control over police policy and practice with police chiefs rather than politicians.

Operationally, policing during the Reform Era underwent dramatic changes. Perhaps most significant, a series of subtle shifts in how preventive patrol was carried out unwittingly yet substantially altered the overall strategy of police. In stages, police first adopted cars, initially for use in transporting prisoners, supervising officers on beats, and taking officers to their beats or from beat to beat. Then as police abandoned foot patrol and turned to patrolling continuously in cars, a new theory of preventive patrol emerged: by rapidly and unpredictably moving through city streets in automobiles, police believed they could create the impression of omnipresence, thus reassuring law-abiding citizens of their availability while deterring potential miscreants and interrupting crimes in progress. Or so the theory went. Capping all this, as telephones and two-way radios became ubiquitous they gave rise to the idea of rapid response by police to citizen calls for service. By the 1960s "full service policing" had come to mean responding to all calls for service within three minutes. Crime prevention was relegated to a small police unit that taught people about locks, alarms, and dogs to deter criminals from breaking in and entering their homes.

With the accumulation of these and other changes, the Anglo Saxon strategy for preventive policing was replaced by a new model of reactive law enforcement—in essence, waiting until a crime had taken place and responding to it. Detectives in local police departments, who built their mystique on the success of the Federal Bureau of Investigation during the 1920s and 1930s, investigated crimes *after* they had been committed and came to epitomize the law enforcement model.[8] The Milwaukee Police Department, for a good share of the twentieth century, was an exemplar of this Reform model. And the model did carry much to commend it: investigating crimes and processing offenders, even after the fact, was certainly important to achieving justice. Reducing intimate contact between police and citizens as well as between police and politicians correspondingly limited opportunities for corruption, inappropriate political interference in policing, and involvement in politics by police. Finally, this new form of policing sought to prevent what many saw as potential dangers raised by police penetrating civil society anonymously and to too great a degree.

Yet by the late 1970s, the Reform model of policing collapsed in the United States. Beginning during the 1960s, crime escalated to unheard of levels—a trend that continued through most of the rest of the century. Research focusing on the mainstays of the Reform model of policing—preventive patrol by automobile and rapid response to calls for service—strongly indicated that these tactics in fact produced little actual benefit for crime control or fear reduction on the part of citizens. Studies of criminal investigation similarly suggested that detectives actually solved few crimes; their main activity consisted of paperwork to prepare cases for court.[9] Minority populations, especially African Americans, became alienated from police, as was clear in the urban unrest of the 1960s. Furthermore, an isolated police culture arose in which many officers frequently were suspicious of, if not openly hostile to, the civilian population. Unfortunately Milwaukee's police department found itself an exemplar of these negative changes as well. It was only with the move to a different strategy of policing, embodied in the community policing model, that police began to address the deterioration in their relationships with citizens in the community and the basic ineffectiveness of their tactics for preventing or reducing crime.

---

8   Walker, 77-78.

9   Braga et al., 4.

THE COMMUNITY POLICING ERA: LATE TWENTIETH/EARLY TWENTY-FIRST CENTURY

During the 1980s, an alternative approach to policing slowly began to develop throughout the country. Proponents of this model sought to restore the basic Anglo Saxon principles of policing a democracy with a focus on neighborhoods and neighborhood problems, community involvement, an emphasis on crime prevention, and transparency in police activities. The notion of a basic responsibility on the part of citizens to be involved in maintaining order, civility, and safety in their community, and the requirement of their consent and support for policing activities re-emerged. By the mid-1990s evidence began to accumulate suggesting that this new mode of policing, coupled with the development of strategic approaches to address specific crime problems and technological advances in data compilation and analysis, could produce dramatic outcomes in preventing and reducing crime.[10]

Since the early 1980s, the term "community policing" has been used to describe these changes taking place in policing, particularly in the United States, although the movement has spread to Europe and beyond. Commonly referred to as a philosophy of policing, community policing has been applied loosely to everything including officer friendly programs, storefront mini-stations, police walk and talk, bicycle patrols, police attending neighborhood meetings, citizen police academies, DARE (drug abuse resistance education), community relations, and many other such activities conducted by police. Yet it is important to recognize that the implementation of such programs or activities does not in and of itself constitute community policing, even though these programs may be worthwhile in their own right and indicative of movement towards community policing. In fact, each of the programs mentioned above could be adopted as an add-on in a department that is actually maintaining a traditional response-oriented law enforcement strategy. Such programs are often used as showpieces to assuage or deflect community and political criticism, especially from minorities. On the other hand, their use within a department that practices community policing is a fundamentally different

---

10   See for example Franklin E. Zimring, *The City that Became Safe: New York's Lessons for Urban Crime and its Control* (New York: Oxford University Press, 2013).

undertaking: here they will not be mere peripheral add-ons, but central to policing operations.

What is it then that constitutes community policing? The chapters that follow offer a detailed examination and examples of the implementation of community policing, especially in Milwaukee. Here we provide an overview of three basic elements that a police department must embrace if it is truly committed to community policing: *crime prevention*—an orientation around crime prevention and the promotion of quality of life and public safety instead of reactive policing; *problem solving*—a focus upon crime as discrete or linked problems that must be addressed rather than on individual crime incidents alone; and finally, *partnerships*—that is, partnering with other law enforcement and non-law enforcement actors and groups in identifying and addressing crime problems. These elements are in many ways tied together and overlap. Let us explore each briefly.

Preventing Crime

As we have seen, American police shifted their approach to crime control profoundly during the 1930s-1960s era. Their earlier approach, based on Anglo Saxon policing in England, had focused on preventing crime through police presence in neighborhoods where police would reduce opportunities for crime and persuade people to behave. During the Reform Era, the emphasis on automobile patrol, responding to calls for service, and the primacy of the detective role in policing constituted a basic move away from prevention to an after-the-fact law enforcement model. In community policing the mission or primary focus of the department is once again on preventing crime and mitigating damage to individuals and society rather than responding to crime after it has taken place. Responding to crimes once they have been committed does nothing to prevent the damage that has affected individual victims and communities.

This does not mean that solving crimes and holding offenders accountable is unimportant. And clearly law enforcement does prevent some future crime by imprisoning current offenders and intimidating would-be offenders. But practitioners of community policing go beyond this: they utilize a wide array of tactics that also target the prevention and reduction of crime. For example, police may work with probation officers to make sure that youthful offenders are obeying the conditions of their probation, attending school, and receiving the support they need to avoid re-offending. Beat officers on the streets pick up on information from local residents and merchants about conflicts brewing between individuals or groups of youth, and collaborate with youth workers to defuse potentially volatile situations. Or police may hear from residents that one house in a neighborhood has recently been the locus of increasing traffic, suggesting that it is becoming a drug or prostitution nexus—and then police devise a plan to address the problem before it escalates and harms the neighborhood more seriously. As each of these scenarios indicates, community policing is centered on crime prevention as well as reduction: stopping the next crime, preventing a few events from becoming a tidal wave, and avoiding future victimization of individuals, families and the community.

Solving Problems

Departments adopting a community policing strategy approach crime not merely in terms of individual cases but as parts of larger crime problems that exist within a particular context.[11] A number of shootings near a local park may be tied to drug dealing at that location. Fear can drive residents away, contributing to a decline in social control that might otherwise operate effectively: parents no longer feel safe bringing their children to the park, older retired people won't pass part of the day there conversing on park benches, workers walk around the park rather than through it when coming home at night, children avoid the area on the way to school, and even community events may move elsewhere. If gangs and turf disputes are involved, violence may escalate and spill over into surrounding streets and residences. A police department committed to community policing will see its responsibility going beyond apprehending specific drug dealers in the park. Instead, it will work to identify and address those problems that allow illegal activity to flourish there and take steps to improve public order and safety that will help local residents reclaim the park.

Community policing organizations do not necessarily assume that the only public safety and crime issues worthy of attention and problem solving are those involving violent crime. Rather, police have learned to listen to the perceptions and concerns of residents and other community members in neighborhoods and to take them seriously. Historically, the priorities of residents and police were often at odds,

---

11   See Herman Goldstein, "Improving Policing: A Problem Solving Approach," *Crime and Delinquency* (April 1979): 236-258.

with citizens concerned about minor offenses and police about felonies. With recent research about the impact of low-level crime on the integrity of neighborhoods and its linkage with an influx of more violent crime, police no longer dismiss such concerns.[12] This does not mean that citizens and citizen groups should always determine police priorities; it does mean that citizen concerns must be taken into account and acted on in some fashion.

Departments committed to community policing and solving crime problems also operate through organizational structures and processes congruent with their mission. Typically they organize their operations and basic units geographically, around neighborhoods and communities. This represents a change from the Reform Era when reliance on automobile patrol and response time caused most police departments to structure beats and districts (precincts) using algorithms based upon desired response time, travel speed and distance, and officer workload. Most departments virtually ignored natural neighborhoods and environmental boundaries such as rivers and major highways. Community policing carried out through effective problem solving recognizes that several factors require geographic organization. Crime tends to be local—criminals like to operate in familiar territory near where they live—and crime problems tend to be neighborhood specific. Geographically organized police departments can pinpoint managerial accountability at the district/precinct level: when police are held accountable for "their" territory, results are often positive. Finally, community groups frequently are organized along neighborhood and natural boundaries, and citizens and community groups are among the most important partners police can and must have if they are to succeed in preventing crime and solving problems related to crime and public safety.

Working in Partnerships

Community policing, as indicated by its very use of the term "community," seeks partners to identify and address public safety problems. This principle has its origins in the Anglo Saxon tradition of citizens policing themselves. Even though complete self-policing is inconceivable in a highly urbanized and suburbanized society, we still expect

12   Anthony A. Braga and Brenda J. Bond, "Policing Crime and Disorder Hot Spots: A Randomized Controlled Trial," *Criminology* 46, (3) (2008): 577-607.

that citizens should not be merely passive recipients of protective services. Rather, in a democracy they bear a social responsibility and hold an explicit obligation to participate in crime control on public streets and in their neighborhoods. Their participation is essential to maintain levels of public order and safety sufficient for a civil society to function.

Police departments committed to community policing recognize that police cannot solve problems alone. Instead, they must continually seek and work with partners—citizens and citizen groups, government agencies from many levels, parts of the justice system and beyond, private sector organizations, and social service and health providers—to identify, prioritize, and resolve problems. In so doing, police maintain their legitimacy and credibility within the community, and share the responsibility for maintaining public safety. But they also strengthen the arsenal of creative and effective tools that can be utilized in problem-solving efforts: the application of civil law as well as criminal, the moral authority of clergy, the resources available from health and service providers and non-profit organizations, a business improvement district's capacity for cleaning up and maintaining order in commercial areas, contacts with schools and trained counselors, and the ability of probation officers and youth leaders to reach young people before they offend or re-offend, to name but a few.

Successful problem-solving efforts ranging from re-establishing order in New York City's subway to reducing homicide in Newark to gang control in Los Angeles, have all depended upon police finding and working with appropriate partners. In the New York City subway, painting graffiti on trains was identified as one of the illegal acts contributing to an environment in which crime and disorder were flourishing. Working with personnel responsible for maintenance in the subway, police devised a policy mandating that every train would be cleaned immediately once it been painted and would not be permitted back in service until this had taken place, thereby removing the incentive for "taggers" to paint the trains.[13] To address the high number of homicides in Newark, police partnered not only with criminal justice agencies but representatives of the faith and social service communities. Meetings were held at local churches, headed by clergy

---

13 Maryalice Sloan-Howitt and George L. Kelling, "Subway Graffiti in New York City: 'Gettin' Up' vs. 'Meanin' It and 'Cleanin' It,'" *Security Journal* 1, no. 3 (1990): 131.

who confronted offenders and told them the local community had had enough and that their neighbors and an array of service providers would support them if they would follow a non-violent path—but they would not tolerate more killing. In Los Angeles, police confronting the problem of gang violence worked with the city attorney's office which turned to civil law and filed injunctions to prevent gang members from congregating in particular areas.[14] To wit, police cannot solely "own" community problems: they need community members and residents as partners because they are policing in a democracy; they need a variety of other partners to enhance their ability to address and solve problems effectively.

Prevention, problem solving, and partnerships are all crucial then to community policing. Yet as should become apparent in the chapters that follow, many more factors contribute to the successful implementation of this form of policing. Leadership, a clear vision of the business of policing, a commitment to accountability and transparency in policing operations, and recognition of the need for training of police officers who routinely exercise a great deal of discretion as they carry out their duties—these too are important facets of community policing. We can see many such qualities in the experiences of the Milwaukee Police Department which has moved into the forefront of community policing in the country.

POLICING IN MILWAUKEE

In the pages that follow, Chapter One documents how I came to work again in Milwaukee and with the police department in 2007 at the behest of the Bradley Foundation. This account focuses especially on my initial assessment of the state of the department and challenges facing the police at that time as well as the community's needs to improve public safety and quality of life.

Chapters Two, Three, and Four chronicle the history of Milwaukee's police department, in many respects a distinguished past, especially during the first half of the twentieth century. Chapter Two begins this history, but focuses primarily upon Milwaukee's police department during the Reform Era. Without a doubt the most important figure in shaping the modern police department was Harold Breier,

---

14 Personal experience from my work with the LAPD during the early 2000s.

chief for twenty years (1964-1984) and arguably Milwaukee's most important police figure of the twentieth century as well as one of its most powerful political forces. Chapters Three and Four document his legacy: Chapter Three examines the relationship of the MPD to Milwaukee's African-American population, an ongoing problem in its history; Chapter Four revisits Breier's link with the MPD's detective culture, recounts his tumultuous relationship with Milwaukee's police union, and treats the MPD's position in developing police theory and practice.

The next two chapters move into the contemporary period. Chapter Five examines Milwaukee's tentative movements towards community policing during the tenures of chiefs who followed Harold Breier. Chapter Six brings us up to date, focusing on the administration of current Chief Edward Flynn—his early successes, controversies that developed during his administration both personally and professionally, and the movement of the MPD into a full community-policing model. Finally, Chapter Seven assesses the achievements of Flynn and the MPD in terms of reducing and preventing crime, firmly establishing community policing and the current position of the MPD within the context of American policing nationally.

CHAPTER ONE

A TIME OF TURMOIL:

MILWAUKEE AND ITS POLICE DEPARTMENT IN 2007

"It's as if Milwaukee, Wis., had reverted to a state of lethal chaos." So began the cover story, "Middle America's Crime Wave" in the December 3, 2006, issue of *Time*. The article continued:

A Special Olympian is killed for his wallet as he waits for a bus. An 11-year-old girl is gang-raped by as many as 19 men. A woman is strangled, her body found burning in a city-owned garbage cart. Twenty-eight people are shot, four fatally, over a holiday weekend.[1]

Milwaukee Archbishop Timothy Dolan lamented: "You'll be able to read about something even more heinous tomorrow."[2] As the Uniform Crime Reports indicate, violent crimes for Milwaukee between 2002 and 2007 increased from 5782 to 8057, or approximately thirty-nine per cent.[3] The factors that give rise to increases or decreases in crime are complicated, often vary by city and state, and are subject to considerable debate. Be that as it may, Milwaukee's increases in crime rates came at a time when the national discussion about crime had gone through substantial change. By 2007, the dramatic crime declines in New York City and Los Angeles dominated the discussion. If those cities, why not others? Under such circumstances it was inevitable that the demand for substantial crime reductions in Milwaukee would

---

1 Kathleen Kingsbury, "Middle America's Crime Wave," *Time* (December 3, 2006).

2 Ibid.

3 Daily Crime Statistics, *Uniform Crime Reporting Statistics*, Federal Bureau of Investigation, U.S. Department of Justice, 1997-2012.

intensify. After all this was *Milwaukee*, noted for its relatively low crime rate and the quality of its police leadership for many decades in the twentieth century.[4]

Late in 2006, Janet Riordan, Director of Community Programs at the Lynde and Harry Bradley Foundation, approached me to discuss Milwaukee's distressing crime situation. Although based in Milwaukee and having a special interest in local issues, the Foundation is recognized nationally as a politically conservative organization. It describes itself as supporting "limited, competent government; a dynamic marketplace for economic, intellectual, and cultural activity; and a vigorous defense, at home and abroad, of American ideas and institutions."[5] Foundation staff at the time had come to believe that crime threatened virtually all of their projects in the city. A strong supporter of charter schools, the Foundation was especially wary of threats to its efforts in education.

I had had limited contact with the Bradley Foundation prior to this time. During the early 1990s it gave me a small grant to cover travel expenses while I was doing research for *Fixing Broken Windows*, a book co-authored with my colleague and wife, Catherine Coles. I had also met Daniel Schmidt, Vice President of Programs, during trips to South and Central America where I lectured and provided consulting services regarding crime problems as a senior fellow for the Manhattan Institute (a New York City-based conservative think-tank with which I had been affiliated since working with the NYC subway during the late 1980s and early 1990s). Perhaps contributing as well to the Foundation's decision to contact me, the *Time* story credited the broken windows theory with being one of the factors leading to the large crime decline of the 1990s.[6] Consequently in 2007 the Bradley Foundation staff invited me to travel to Milwaukee and meet with

---

4   *Time* highlighted Milwaukee, despite this history, because homicides had increased by 40 percent between 2004 and 2005, the largest percentage increase in the country. This statistic was misleading, however: Milwaukee had a big homicide drop in 2004 and the increase really amounted to a return to pre-2004 trends.

5   The Bradley Foundation, Statement of Mission, www.bradleyfdn.org/.

6   The broken windows theory, about which more is included below, argues for a connection between disorderly behavior and conditions (minor offenses) and more serious offenses. It is an approach widely associated with the crime declines in New York City's subway and later in the city itself. See

them to discuss ongoing violence there, its impact on the city, and any ideas I might have about how the Foundation could help. Given my professional experience, clearly any help I could provide would be in the realm of working with police.

I attended at least two preliminary meetings with Bradley Foundation staff, after which the Foundation agreed to underwrite the cost of consulting services for the city by Robert Wasserman (whose involvement I proposed) and me. Wasserman was well-known in policing circles, had served as a consultant to and staff member of several major police departments in the United States and internationally, and had particular expertise in organizational and administrative issues in policing. I had worked with him from my earliest professional days in Kansas City during the 1970s and in at least a dozen cities since—among them Boston, New York City, and Los Angeles. In 2007, Milwaukee had already begun its search for a new police chief after then-chief Nannette Hegerty announced her plans not to seek reappointment. I believed it would be important that we provide advice in the selection process and Wasserman also could offer help to the city in identifying appropriate candidates.

CONSULTING WITH A NEW ANGLE: PROBLEM SOLVING TO IMPROVE POLICING AND REDUCE CRIME IN MILWAUKEE

The offer of our services to the city was not accepted without caution, at least initially. Milwaukee's mayor since 2004, Tom Barrett, was a Democrat and the conservative reputation of the Foundation was well known. If not a cause for concern to the mayor, this reputation appeared to trouble some of his staff. Similarly my own reputation raised hackles among many liberals: I had influenced the operations of the New York City Police Department (NYPD) under the administration of Republican Mayor Rudy Giuliani and often had been portrayed (inaccurately from my point of view) as an advocate of tough, "zero tolerance" police tactics. Nonetheless, after several meetings the mayor and his staff became receptive to the offer of our services and arranged for us to meet with the city's Common Council President

---

James Q. Wilson and George L. Kelling, "The Police and Neighborhood Safety," *The Atlantic* (March 1982).

Willie Hines as well as the Fire and Police Commission—the latter the city's police policy-making authority. Both agreed to our involvement.[7] It is typical for hired consultants to go into police departments, study them, and as a final step submit reports to the agency that hired them. Wasserman and I, individually and together, had done this several times. Most of these reports are received, praised, and then ignored. Milwaukee has several such documents on file, written by other consultants. I was no longer prepared to consult in this fashion, especially after my experiences in the New York City subway during the late 1980s and early 1990s. There, at the behest of Chair of the New York State Transportation Authority Robert Kiley, Wasserman and I collected data, produced a report, and attended the farewell luncheon put on by the Transit Police Department. Surprisingly, however, Chairperson Kiley was not ready to let us leave and have the report languish. From his point of view the future of the subway system was severely threatened by disorder and crime, and police seemed unwilling or incapable of dealing with it. Instead, he commissioned me to do something about it. *Fixing Broken Windows* recounts the details of what happened next in the subway system, as does *New Yorker* writer Malcolm Gladwell's book, *Tipping Point*.[8] Apart from the outcome, the experience itself changed my approach to consulting: from a report and recommendation writer to an active problem solver in every project I took on in the future.

"Consultant for solving problems" is the role I have undertaken since—in New York City, Boston, and Los Angeles. For example, when William Bratton became chief in Los Angeles, he and Mayor Hahn asked me to deal with several problems: gangs and drug dealing in MacArthur Park, prostitution in Hollywood, disorder on skid row, and gangs in the South District and the Valley. Likewise, one of my most recent periods of consultation was in Boston where I was asked to help deal with the problem of "street people" around Boston's Common and Garden after gang members put a bullet through a

---

7   I continued to work with the MPD from 2007 to 2010. Robert Wasserman worked from 2007 to 2009. Many of our specific activities are detailed in the chapters that follow.

8   George L. Kelling and Catherine M. Coles, *Fixing Broken Windows: Restoring Order and Reducing Crime in Our Communities* (New York: The Free Press, 1996); Malcolm Gladwell, *The Tipping Point: How Little Things Can Make a Big Difference* (New York: Back Bay Books, 2000).

window of the adjacent state capital building. From the beginning in Milwaukee I made clear, first to the Bradley Foundation and later to city and police officials, that this would be the model for involvement by Wasserman and me: not report writing, but active problem solving. Wasserman would deal with organizational and administrative issues in the police department while I addressed police policies and activities in the community.

The overarching problem, of course, was how to impact crime itself. More than anything else, Milwaukee police officials seemed to believe that they were doing the best they could. Among the city's many problems—Milwaukee at that time was classified as one of the most racially segregated cities in the U.S. and among those with the highest poverty rate—crime was viewed as yet another negative about which not much could be done. And in some respects the police department itself did not appear to be doing too badly: its homicide clearance rate was among the highest in the country; as a result of efforts by former chiefs Arreola, Jones, and Hegerty, more minorities and women had been hired and were moving up through the ranks; MPD was attempting to reach out to neighborhoods and community partners; and Chief Hegerty had improved administrative processes (for example, training, recruitment, and discipline). Yet as then Chair of the Milwaukee Fire and Police Commission Leonard Sobczak put it: "There simply was a sense of hopelessness when it came to crime. The view was police were improving: they were doing the best they could; Milwaukeeans just had to live with crime—it was beyond police control."[9] Clearly many in the city did not accept this last assumption; nor did I.

FIRST STEPS: GETTING A "TAKE" ON THE STATE OF POLICING IN MILWAUKEE

As Wasserman and I became intensively involved in Milwaukee, I began gathering information from a number of sources to expand my understanding of the city's problems with policing and crime. I talked with Bradley Foundation staff, Mayor Barrett and his staff, and Milwaukee contacts that I had maintained over the years. I looked at extant studies of the MPD. And I tried to glean information concerning the professional reputation of the MPD among other police departments and leaders and Milwaukee's media.

---

9   Leonard Sobczak, interview by George Kelling, March 6, 2013.

A number of issues emerged that would need to be addressed as we devised a plan for working with the police department. Some represented challenges growing out of relatively recent events, including repercussions emanating from the early resignation of Chief Hegerty, the lack of a clear mission for the police department, and the sad state of the MPD's information technology. Other problems were longer standing: the dominance of the MPD's detective culture (a holdover from an earlier approach to policing) and ongoing racial tensions both within the MPD and in its relationship to the community. While needing immediate attention, these matters would demand an ongoing commitment from the next chief in Milwaukee. And, of course, the search for a new police chief, already underway, loomed large in our assessment. I treat briefly here, and in greater detail in subsequent chapters, each of the issues that we knew the next chief would face as well as the selection process itself.

Changing Leadership in the MPD: Chief Hegerty's Resignation

As I began working in Milwaukee, perhaps the most unsettling initial circumstance was Police Chief Nannette Hegerty's prior announcement not to seek a second term, made almost a year in advance of completing her first term. Mayor John Norquist had appointed Hegerty to a four-year term in November 2003, before resigning himself in January 2004. Hegerty went on to serve the rest of her term in office under Mayor Tom Barrett (who was elected in April 2004); but in January 2007, she announced that she would resign effective at the end of her term in November of that year. It is not clear whether Mayor Barrett would have reappointed Hegerty. At minimum, Barrett wanted to conduct a national search to ensure that Milwaukee had the best possible chief during his continued mayoral tenure. If Hegerty had wanted to stay, she would have had to compete in such a search.

By most accounts, Hegerty was a successful chief of police who was viewed favorably by the Barrett administration. She was widely admired by community groups; was a strong disciplinarian who tore down the "blue curtain" that surrounded the infamous Frank Jude case;[10] was generally thought to have improved the department's

---

10   Frank Jude was a bi-racial civilian who was savagely beaten and tortured by white on- and off-duty police officers after Jude was accused of stealing an officer's badge at a party. State and local prosecutions followed, but Hegerty conducted thorough investigations, fired nine officers, suspended

morale; and at least initially, was credited with declining crime rates, although homicides went up and down during her administration. Hegerty herself identified her major contributions as implementing in-car technology (video cameras, two-finger identification systems, and automatic traffic ticket writing), creating a Police Foundation (an organizational location for private monies to be donated for police purposes, such as reestablishing a canine unit), stabilizing the disciplinary system, and raising hiring standards—all of which she believed would have positive long-term impacts on the MPD.[11]

Hegerty's early announcement of her intent to leave meant that she would stay in office for ten months as a lame duck chief. In respects, being a lame duck is not unusual in American policing as the tenure of chiefs is often quite short and everyone including chiefs, politicians and unions, are well aware of this. Some chiefs serve at the pleasure of a mayor or a commission, others get contracts—regardless, life as a chief can be quite short.[12] What was worrisome and ultimately unsettling was not just that Hegerty announced her resignation so early, but that she abdicated leadership during her remaining tenure, a view held by many in the department. During her last ten months in office, Hegerty largely handed the MPD over to deputy and assistant chiefs, especially the deputy chief who headed the Criminal Investigation Bureau (CIB). I met Chief Hegerty only once before Wasserman and I started to consult formally, at a meeting of the Fire and Police Commission. Insofar as I know she made no objection to our involvement. However, when I attempted to set up a meeting with her after the Fire and Police Commission approved our work, her support staff diverted me to assistant and deputy chiefs. It appeared at the time that she had already withdrawn from key areas of administration.

---

three, and demoted one. Drew Olson, "Police Chief's Resignation Causes Reverberations," *On Milwaukee*, January 6, 2007.

11 Nannette Hegerty (chief of the MPD), post-exit interview by Deputy Inspector (Ret.) Craig Hasting, 2009, Milwaukee Police Department Historical Society. Many current high-level MPD staff members, who were mid-managers when Hegerty was chief, would dispute some of Hegerty's claims, especially with regard to improving departmental uses of technology.

12 Although exact data are hard to come by, a three-year tenure as a chief of police is not short in American terms; most chiefs serve approximately this length of time.

In fact, Chief Hegerty would state later that she viewed her decision to announce her retirement so early as the major mistake of her
administration. She indicated that her intention had been to give the
Fire and Police Commission ample time to find a competent replace-
ment while she was still in office. In this manner she could assist her
successor by bringing her/him up to date on the primary issues confronting the department and introducing the new chief to contacts she
had made during her administration.[13] Others, especially those who
moved into senior positions in the MPD's subsequent administration,
saw the consequences of her actions as largely negative.[14] For them the
early announcement and abdication of authority exacerbated the normal jockeying that goes on among senior managers during transition
periods. Indeed, several senior administrators were eager to succeed
Hegerty—which was not at all surprising. But given the length of time
and the power vacuum that ensued, many senior managers aggressively attempted to line up support among other senior as well as mid-level managers. Local politicians also had their favorites.

For most of the mid-managers who were to become future leaders
of the MPD, the length of Hegerty's lame duck administration worsened an already problematic relationship between the Patrol Bureau
and CIB. As it was, the head of the Criminal Intelligence Bureau was
considered to have the inside track to become the next chief. When
Hegerty put the Patrol Bureau under the leadership of someone recruited from CIB rather than from the Patrol Bureau itself, many senior members of the Patrol Bureau saw these factors as the handwrit-
ing on the wall: Patrol would continue to be the MPD's organizational
stepchild. Additionally, Chief Hegerty's announced retirement froze
MPD personnel in place for almost a year. No sooner had Hegerty
made public her intention not to seek a second term than the city's
personnel director announced that no further promotions to MPD's
exempt positions (captains and above are exempt from civil service)
would be approved until a new chief had been appointed. This step
certainly was appropriate, reserving for the new chief the freedom
to designate his/her senior staff. Nevertheless given that a new chief
(especially an outsider) would likely need several months to create a
management team, the legitimate career aspirations of many officers

13 Hegerty post-exit interview.

14 MPD Command staff group, interview by George Kelling, December
17, 2012.

were effectively put on hold for an extended period and perhaps even ended for some.

Moreover, Hegerty's premature announcement led to certain actions that should have been delayed until a new chief was in office. Redistricting was one example. Given Milwaukee's changing demographic and crime patterns, Hegerty decided it was time to draw much-needed new police district boundaries. And, given the assumptions that guide district makeup and the amount of effort that must be expended in district construction, redistricting was too important to take place during a lame duck or transition period. Yet the department went ahead with redistricting. Wasserman and I felt so strongly about this issue that we approached the mayor and his staff to see if we could get them to block it. Unfortunately we were unsuccessful.

The Lack of Clear Mission for the MPD

A second issue that emerged early on in my work with the MPD was the lack of clarity about a basic mission to guide members of the department, and police policy and activities in the community. A clear policing mission "brands" the organization in the eyes of the community, setting out the values and goals of the department in its dealings with citizens as well as other partners in crime control efforts. Internally, a mission guides police managers and officers themselves, both in formal terms in setting priorities and carrying out specified roles and activities and informally as police exercise discretion in all their daily work. In the absence of an explicit mission, the basic tactics that the MPD utilized and held up to measure its performance implicitly reflected an outdated model of policing that had largely been discredited by the late twentieth century. By most accounts, response time to calls for service dominated the department's thinking about quality police service. Crime and disorder levels were certainly among the metrics that top staff used to evaluate district and unit commanders, but it was clear that they were in the second or even third tier of departmental concerns. I found ample evidence for these conclusions from three main sources: minutes taken of the quarterly evaluations of district and unit commands; conversations with departmental leaders, especially district commanders; and a 2007 report, *Patrol Resource*

Analysis of the Police Department: Milwaukee, Wisconsin, authorized by Milwaukee's Fire and Police Commission.[15]

Assistant and/or deputy chiefs generally conducted quarterly evaluations of district commanders and unit heads. Many in the MPD perceived these meetings as the equivalent of "compstat," the accountability/crime analysis and tactical planning meetings developed in New York City during the 1990s that subsequently became a model for implementing the problem-solving approach increasingly utilized in American policing. In compstat meetings (with which Wasserman and I both had first-hand experience in New York City and elsewhere), crime data are presented and analyzed in considerable detail: who is doing what to whom, where, when, and why; and what police are doing or could do to stop it. Implicit in such analyses is the awareness that crime is multifaceted and comprised of a complex set of problems. Legal terms such as "homicide" or "burglary" tell us little about what is really transpiring; the broadest term "crime" tells us even less. For example, car theft can be carried out as joyriding by teens, a theft for parts, a kidnapping, a theft to ship overseas, for simple transportation, or to use in commission of other crimes. Every category of crime—homicide, assault, burglary—is the same: each represents a complex set of behaviors that often cluster in "hot spots" or "hot times" in particular neighborhoods. The specific nature of problems, in turn, requires that responses, even within the same legal category, vary considerably: police will no doubt address juveniles joy riding in stolen cars in a different fashion than they will professional thieves stealing cars to resell their parts.

Yet as reflected in the minutes of quarterly evaluations, little time was spent in such analyses by the MPD in 2007. Instead the most common concerns were response time, control of overtime, use of sick time, attendance at in-service training, and similar administrative concerns. District commanders generally reported that they did or did not achieve the routinely established goals in crime reduction and the discussion moved on to other matters. Specified goals were generally quite minimal: reduce crime by .5% to 2 percent, reduce response time by forty-five seconds, reduce overtime, and so on. The point is, when reviewing these minutes it would be hard to decipher the real business

15 Matrix Consulting Group, *Patrol Resource Analysis of the Police Department: Milwaukee, Wisconsin* (unpublished report, November 8, 2007).

of the MPD. Moreover the discussions offered no sense of urgency for addressing Milwaukee's crime problems.

From a second source—conversations with district captains and other mid-managers—similar findings regarding the absence of a policing mission and use of out-of-date tactics emerged. As far as most of these officials were concerned, whether explicit in the evaluations or not, their business was to keep response time low and reduce use of overtime. The view that short response time is important is based on the premise that it is helpful in preventing crime, satisfying citizens, and making good arrests. Despite the intuitive appeal of this premise, however, research has convincingly demonstrated that short response time is a highly overrated indicator of quality police performance (an issue touched upon in the Introduction and which is addressed in greater detail in a subsequent chapter). Similarly, the 2007 Matrix Report, while in some ways a valuable document that illustrated an understanding of research on police operations as well as ways to increase police efficiency and decrease police costs, presented no explicit statement of the basic mission of the MPD.[16] Rather, the department's core business was simply assumed to be rapid response to calls for service and proactive patrol. What no one seemed to acknowledge was that the core business of policing had moved far beyond these mid-twentieth century tactics.

The Lack of Adequate Information Technology

If the core business of policing had changed, the tools needed to support it were also being transformed. In this realm another readily identifiable problem for the MPD lay in its information technology system. Every chief since Phillip Arreola (1989-1996) struggled to get on top of the department's technological problems, both for administrative and tactical purposes; all were largely unsuccessful. Most recently, Milwaukee had purchased (in 2002) and operationalized (in 2005) a computer programming system for MPD that simply did not meet its data management needs. By 2007, both Common Council

---

16   Ibid. The report's discussion of the process by which felony cases are handed off from responding police officers to detectives properly understands the inefficiencies of how this is carried out in most police departments, including Milwaukee. It is often the case that the detectives' preliminary investigations merely replicate the preliminary investigations by the patrol officer without any real gain. Other such examples could be given.

members and the city comptroller's office were expressing concerns
that many important system functions were not operational. The system not only did not work as it should; its vendor failed to improve
it, even though Milwaukee made twenty-two outstanding service requests and paid the vendor another quarter million dollars for modifi-
cations.[17] Furthermore the MPD relied on police staff thought to have
sufficient background in computer science to manage or improve the
system; but clearly they did not. In fact, the primary person responsible for upgrading the system was an MPD captain who negotiated an
ongoing contract after he retired. The MPD did not seek professional
help from Milwaukee's private sector which would have been eager to
be of assistance.

The development and maintenance of computer-based capabilities
for both administrative and tactical purposes is a complicated process.
Nonetheless, technicalities aside, what was apparent from the beginning was that the MPD lacked the capability for monitoring crimes
and problems on a real-time basis, a condition that was required for
an aggressive crime prevention strategy oriented around crime analysis
and problem solving. Operationally MPD's leadership could not have
utilized compstat effectively, even if they had wanted to, since their
inadequate information technology lacked this capacity. Furthermore,
this inadequacy not only limited Milwaukee's crime control capacity
directly, it did so indirectly as well by reducing the ability of senior
managers to hold district and unit commanders accountable. Top
command communicated no sense of urgency to the next level; instead, they gave relatively meaningless admonitions that commanders should reduce response time by a matter of seconds and crime by
trivial amounts. The absence of an effective technological capacity for
collecting, storing, and facilitating analysis of data on local crime and
problems was just one more obstacle to Milwaukee improving its policing organization and effectiveness in the community.

The Dominance of the Detective Culture

While the basic mission of policing in Milwaukee needed to be re-
framed and tools supporting it improved, a serious internal organizational obstacle to progress lay in the persistence in the MPD of what
I call the dominance of the detective culture. Since the 1960s, when I

17   Chief Edward Flynn, power point presentation (Milwaukee Police
     Department, November 29, 2012).

first became familiar with the MPD through its union leaders Robert Kliesmet and Jerry Dudzik I had been aware of its reputation as a department that emphasized detectives and other special units over patrol.[18] This was not unusual in American policing; nevertheless, it represented an approach to policing (the Reform model) largely at odds with the new paradigm that had come to the forefront since the 1990s—community and problem-oriented policing.

Criminal investigation/detective units have much to offer a preventive policing strategy. Detectives have special expertise and skills (such as interviewing) that are invaluable. As part of their work, they can gain valuable perspectives on individual incidents that together comprise a larger crime problem. Such information is crucial to successful problem solving: meaningful crime analysis and crafting of tactics that will be effective for addressing problems both depend upon detective input into the entire effort. Unfortunately, in the MPD at this time (2007), detectives' roles remained rooted in the reactive law enforcement/arrest orientation of the past, when they were seen as elite professionals carrying out the core mission of the organization and patrol officers as mere "grunts" who dealt with residual problems. Elevating the role of detectives in this way allowed organizational misperceptions to continue. In particular, the central organizational role and work of patrol officers—problem solving on the ground and being in constant contact with citizens in neighborhoods—were demeaned and the often-pedestrian activities of detectives undeservedly enhanced. The primary problem with detectives would not be any lack of capability, but their reluctance to work collaboratively within the police department to prevent crime in ways other than criminal investigation.

A second concern about detectives and special units in the MPD lay in the potential for cronyism—that is, giving preferential appointments to friends or colleagues for reasons other than merit. Not only can cronyism be used by cliques or groups in detective units to maintain advantageous positions and perks (such as money, prestige, steady shifts, and access to promotions), it can also function to keep other persons or groups out, especially minorities or women. In Milwaukee by 2007, an assignment to detective was a formal promotion governed by civil service. Nevertheless, up until the late 1970s, one had first to

18 Special units such as SWAT (Special Weapons and Tactics) and Intelligence were held in high esteem.

be an acting detective for a year before being eligible to take the civil service exam for detective. Favoritism rather than merit could and did control appointment to acting detective status, thereby effectively determining who was eligible to take the civil service exam.[19] Many in the MPD believed this strategy was employed to keep the few minorities in the department from becoming full detectives: maintaining the appearance of having them serve as detectives or in assignments for which race was important (such as undercover work) by appointing them to acting positions, but reassigning them before they served a full year and qualified to take the civil service examination. Former police union head Robert Kliesmet describes the entire promotional system in the MPD during this time as a "godfather" process because of cronyism implicit in the "acting" requirement.[20]

Elitism and cronyism gave rise to deep divisions in the MPD that impacted not just minorities and women but were felt throughout the organization. Even with the change in procedures for attaining detective status, generations of detectives had benefited from the system to the exclusion of others with legitimate claims based on merit. And detective units that became elite power groups were difficult to dislodge. Having access to certain information, they could form mutually advantageous relations with media, politicians, and other powerful people and groups in a community. Many chiefs in Milwaukee and elsewhere had run headlong into the protective power represented by detectives and/or their units.

To the extent that detectives (and other special units) were embraced as the elite among Milwaukee police, then, the shift to a twenty-first century community policing paradigm would be forestalled. Both Wasserman and I recognized that the persistence of this culture and its detrimental effects would likely lead to some resistance toward change in the department that would not be easily or quickly overcome.

Issues of Race and Gender
Despite the intentions of three chiefs of police—Arreola (1989-96), Jones (1996-2003), and Hegerty (2003-2007)—to end both the

---

19 I have tried to determine the exact date of this change; however, the Fire and Police Commission was unable to be more specific than "late 1970s."

20 Robert Kliesmet (former MPD officer and head of the Milwaukee PPA), interview by George Kelling, January 28, 2011.

discord between police and minorities inside the department as well as a strained relationship between the MPD and minority groups in the community, problems persisted until well into the twenty-first century. The MPD's history of dealing with minorities was not unusual among police departments. Recruiting, hiring, and promoting minorities really were not issues for departments until President Lyndon Johnson's Commission on Law Enforcement and the Administration of Justice called them to public attention in the 1960s. In 1960, the MPD hired ninety-six police officers: two African Americans, no Hispanics, and no Native Americans. No women were hired until 1975 when twelve joined the MPD. And, as in many other cities, the transition was tumultuous. In 1974, Milwaukee entered into a consent decree mandating that two of every five new hires would be minorities and one of every five women of any race.[21]

Although I detail many of the following events in subsequent chapters, suffice it to say here that the MPD lurched from one crisis to another regarding minorities and women from the 1960s forward: beginning with a chief whose insinuating comments about race distanced the MPD from minorities; through a series of tragic deaths of persons in police custody; to legal challenges that led to the consent decree; through the cases of serial killer Jeffrey Dahmer and Frank Jude (who was beaten by police officers). Race and gender disputes spilled into the twenty-first century, even at the highest levels. In 2002, Chief Arthur Jones, an African American, filed a racial discrimination suit against the City of Milwaukee. In 2005, a federal jury awarded seventeen officers $2.2 million for reverse discrimination by Chief Jones. A new chief in Milwaukee in 2007 would have his/her hands full dealing with race and gender issues in the department and within the community. Our premonitions proved accurate when in 2008, after a new administration began, former chief Nannette Hegerty filed a gender discrimination suit against the city claiming that she was underpaid relative to the salary of her successor, Edward Flynn.

As troublesome as these problems might have been, I believed that the MPD still had a lot going for it. Mayor Tom Barnett, Council President Willie Hines, and Fire and Police Chair Len Sobczak were all enthusiastic about strengthening the MPD and willing to take advice about how to proceed. Although budget problems loomed for

---

21 Consent decree, United States of America v. City of Milwaukee (No. 74-C-480, E.D. Wis., October 17, 1974).

Milwaukee as they did for virtually every American city, there were no serious proposals to cut back on police (although overtime had to be controlled). And difficult as the relationship was between minorities and the MPD, things had not deteriorated to the point that citizens were unwilling to cooperate with the police: "don't snitch" had not gained a strong foothold in Milwaukee. I also saw reason for optimism within the MPD itself. Over the years the department had been adding and promoting talented staff. My early contacts, especially with district commanders, were heartening. There was virtually no opposition to Wasserman and me entering the department as outside consultants; it was as if almost everyone in the MPD knew that they had to change. At the same time an undercurrent of dissatisfaction was evident within the department about how the MPD was doing professionally—a feeling powerful enough that police seemed prepared to accept an outstanding outsider as a new chief.

THE SEARCH FOR A NEW POLICE CHIEF

Both Robert Wasserman and I believed in 2007 that the single most important thing we could accomplish in Milwaukee would be to help the city find the best chief of police possible. At the time we became involved as consultants, Milwaukee had entered the last stages of selecting finalists. Sixteen had been identified: eight from inside the MPD and an equal number from outside. Neither Wasserman nor I knew any of the internal candidates—none had reputations outside of Milwaukee. Based on their resumes and written statements, many appeared to have promise, but they simply did not appear ready to run a department the size of Milwaukee's. Few reflected in-depth familiarity with the major movements in policing or public sector management, and several of the most promising candidates had spent most of their careers in specialized units, especially the detective unit. Although not a disqualifying criterion in itself, given Milwaukee's reputation as having a detective-dominated culture and the problems we saw this causing, we worried about perpetuating the culture.

We did know some of the outside candidates and were not impressed with their backgrounds or future possibilities. Several were retired mid-managers from larger police departments looking to finish their careers in a smaller, "easier" city. We were particularly concerned about the capabilities of outside candidates because of a rule of thumb that guided our thinking about police chief selection: if a department was on the right track in the eyes of community stakeholders, all other things being equal an internal candidate should be strongly considered. On the other hand, if a department was underperforming (again assuming all other things to be equal), an outside candidate should be given primacy. Milwaukee's circumstances suggested to us that an outsider might be the best candidate to become chief. Our immediate concern then was to enrich the pool so that if the Fire and Police Commission and Mayor Barrett sought to reach outside of the MPD for a chief, very strong candidates would be available. Consequently, we urged them to reopen the search process.

Wasserman had had extensive experience in such recruitment processes. His point of view was that a city the size of Milwaukee should not only run an open process for both insiders and outsiders, but should actively encourage outstanding external candidates to apply. By outstanding external candidates he meant second or third level administrators (such as deputy or assistant chiefs) in large departments like New York, Los Angeles, or Chicago, or chiefs in medium-sized cities like Madison, Wisconsin, or Portland, Maine—in other words, officials with extensive experience in senior administrative positions. Wasserman suggested specifically that city officials extend invitations to at least two chiefs from medium-sized cities to apply for the Milwaukee position, with two caveats: they would have to go through the entire application process, and no assurance would be given that they would be selected as a finalist or appointed chief. One of those he recommended was Edward Flynn, Chief of Police in Springfield, Massachusetts.

I was enthusiastic about Flynn, having first met him professionally in the mid-1990s when he was the Chief of Police in Chelsea, Massachusetts. From there he had moved to head the Arlington, Virginia Police Department in 1998; later served as the Massachusetts Director of Public Safety under Governor Mitt Romney (beginning in 2003); and finally became commissioner in Springfield in 2006. I was impressed by his grasp of the police literature and his ability to articulate police knowledge and research. He seemed to be one of a number of highly regarded police officials garnering attention and moving up on the national scene. In my mind he was ready to head a large police department. Wasserman and I decided that I would contact Flynn, which I did. Although at first reluctant to move since he had been in Springfield for only eighteen months—as his application became public, he feared it would jeopardize his credibility and future there—Flynn did apply. He was named chief on November 15, 2007, and sworn in as Milwaukee's seventeenth chief and second "outside" chief on January 7, 2008.

Later in this account we will return to an examination of Chief Flynn's record in office, to assess his progress and that of the department under his leadership for the past few years. But, before continuing that tale, it is fair to ask: "What happened in all the decades that preceded Chief Flynn's administration?" In Chapter Two we examine how and why the MPD, once a highly emulated police department, fell out of its position as a leading American police department.

CHAPTER TWO

THE DEVELOPMENT OF POLICING IN MILWAUKEE: THE REFORM ERA AND HAROLD BREIER

By the end of the twentieth century, areas of Milwaukee as in many American cities were terror zones: children could not play in front of their homes or in parks, churches and schools could not function, commerce was strangled, and residents struggled daily to protect their children, themselves, and their property from predators. What happened during the 1960s, 1970s, and 1980s so that in many public spaces and neighborhoods having to tolerate the intolerable had become the "normal" state of affairs? How is it that carrying guns and killing each other became customary for youths in these areas? How did we lose control?

High levels of crime, whether in Milwaukee or elsewhere, at any given time are neither inevitable nor the natural state of affairs. But during the period discussed here a confluence of factors produced what was, in effect, a perfect storm. Beginning in the 1950s new approaches to social policies and practices became central to government policy and practice. Soon after, an era of cultural reform emerged that emphasized and protected the rights of individuals while ignoring those of neighborhoods and communities. While well intentioned, taken together these forces nonetheless proved destructive to many local communities, leading to a breakdown of norms and social controls that had previously operated to help keep crime in check. Changes in policing that removed officers from neighborhood streets and caused them to respond to crime rather than help prevent it meant that they were increasingly ineffective. Milwaukee experienced many of the negative effects of these changes—one being a dramatic rise in crime that tested police and citizens alike.

This chapter examines Milwaukee's police department during this time of tumultuous change. Few Milwaukeeans remember or appreciate the prestige of the Milwaukee Police Department during the first half the twentieth century. Until well past World War II, MPD was preeminent among American police departments—one of *the* national models for what came to be known as professional policing. Two chiefs bookend this crucial period of policing in Milwaukee: John Janssen and Harold Breier. Chief Janssen served for thirty-three years, from 1888–1921; Chief Breier for twenty years, from 1964–1984. Chief Janssen ushered in the Reform (or professional) Era of policing both in Milwaukee and nationally; Chief Breier brought it to a close in Milwaukee, although other cities around the country continued to struggle with the reform strategy. Both were honest, independent, authoritarian, powerful, and unaccountable to either the general public or political leaders. Neither brooked any challenge to his views about policing or administration. In large part, it was Milwaukee itself that gave such power to the office, for the city was one of the first to protect chiefs from politics and thereby termination without cause. With an ordinance passed in 1885, Janssen became the first chief with lifetime tenure both in Milwaukee and the United States; Breier would be the last Milwaukee chief to enjoy this status.

Harold Breier is clearly the singular policing figure in this narrative: his impact on the Milwaukee Police Department lasted well beyond his departure in 1984 and remained apparent in 2007. Yet he and the police department, with its orientation around Reform Era strategies and tactics, were fundamentally flawed when it came to meeting many of the challenges that arose beginning in mid-century. Eventually the community policing movement that followed would prove more effective, both in addressing crime and gaining the support of citizens. But first we must understand just what happened to propel police—and Milwaukee—to such high and low points during the twentieth century.

AN OVERVIEW OF MILWAUKEE POLICING

Substantively Milwaukee policing was typical of American cities during the late 1800s. In founding its police department in 1855, Milwaukee, like Boston and New York City earlier, patterned its force after London's Metropolitan Police. In London, police were to maintain order, prevent crime, and provide services; their methods were patrolling neighborhoods, seeking public approval, and using minimum force. In contrast with the London Metropolitan police who received their authority directly from the crown, police in the United States were overlaid on the urban ward "boss" system that characterized cities during much of the nineteenth into the twentieth centuries. Here policing was entirely a local matter. The strength of such an arrangement was that it kept police close to local citizens and their concerns; the weakness was that it led to corruption and political manipulation of police departments.

In this regard Milwaukee was no different—perhaps a little worse—than its older peers in New York and Boston. Tradition has it that prior to Chief Janssen, Milwaukee and its police were so corrupt that trainloads of Chicagoans regularly traveled to Milwaukee for gambling and associated vices.[1] As in most of the United States at the time, the mayor and Common Council would appoint a chief of police; after the next election a new mayor and Common Council would appoint a new chief and his cronies. During the Milwaukee Police Department's first thirty years, eight chiefs rotated through this spoils system. Milwaukee's first chief, William Beck, was appointed on and off three times. Beck, a local farmer who previously had been a New York City Police Department detective, was recruited by Milwaukee County Sheriff Herman Page to serve as deputy and help confront Milwaukee's lawlessness. Although Beck earned a reputation for apprehending a number of thieves, crime and disorder remained such a serious problem in the city that in 1855 aldermen created the Milwaukee Police Department. Mayor James Cross appointed Beck as chief. In 1861, after two riots, Beck resigned. He returned as chief in 1863 for fifteen years, and again in 1880 for two years. Depending on one's politics he was a good guy or bad guy: regardless, such instability shaped Milwaukee's early police.[2]

---

1   John J. McCarthy, "Harold Breier: Imperious, Old-Fashioned and Chief for Life," *Police Magazine* (November 1981). See also, Frederick I. Olson, "Milwaukee's Socialist Mayors: End of an Era and a Beginning," in *Milwaukee Stories,* ed. Thomas J. Jablonsky (Milwaukee: Marquette University Press, 2005), 431.

2   City of Milwaukee website, accessed November 22, 2014, http://www.city.milwaukee.gov/Directory/police/About-MPD/History.

In 1885 the Wisconsin legislature, to counter political manipulation and backed by Mayor Emil Walber, passed legislation creating the Milwaukee Fire and Police Commission—the first such commission in the United States.[3] This four-person, non-partisan body would approve all appointments to Milwaukee's fire and police departments. Moreover, police chiefs would be appointed with lifetime tenure. John Janessen was the first chief appointed under these provisions in 1888. In 1911 further state legislation added to this independence by vesting full authority in Milwaukee's police chief to establish police policies, rules, and regulations—in effect creating a firewall between police departments and elected officials.[4] Milwaukee was now unique and the envy of chiefs throughout the country: no other police department, no other chief, enjoyed such autonomy. For all practical purposes, once appointed a Milwaukee chief not only had lifetime tenure but could completely dictate police priorities, policies, and rules and regulations, and was accountable to no one.

Once Milwaukee's system was in operation, powerful chiefs led lengthy administrations. Janssen had the longest tenure, with Breier only the sixth police chief from 1888 forward. Up through Harold Breier's administration the average tenure was almost ten years. Furthermore, prior to Breier's administration only a single twentieth-century chief ran into difficulty that shortened his tenure: when Howard Johnson (1957-1964), Breier's immediate predecessor, was chief a major corruption scandal involving organized crime and prostitution engulfed the MPD.

After Breier the terms of chiefs dropped to an average of five years. Part of this was due to changing ordinances that put term limits on the position—at first seven years, but later changed to four with the option

---

3   Ibid., accessed Nov. 22, 2014, http://www.city.milwaukee.gov/ImageLibrary/Groups/cityFPC/Reports/FPC_125.pdf. See also Richard Jerome, "Promoting Police Accountability in Milwaukee: Strengthening the Fire and Police Commission" (unpub. report, Police Assessment Resource Center, June 2006).

4   There is some dispute as how much actual authority Milwaukee's Common Council and mayor had over police policies and practices. See, for example, Matthew J. Flynn, "Comment: Police Accountability in Wisconsin," *Wisconsin Law Review* 1974: 1131. Flynn argues that both the Common Council and mayor had more authority than they were prepared to exercise during Harold Breier's reign.

of renewal. But this trend also arose out of unsettled circumstances in the MPD and its political environment. Chief Robert Ziarnik (1984-1989) quit after five years following a conflict with Common Council members. Chief Phillip Arreola (1989-1996) sought but was not appointed to a second term, as occurred too with Chief Arthur Jones (1996-2003). Chief Nannette Hegerty (2003-2007) served her first term but resigned before her reappointment was considered. Finally Chief Edward Flynn (2008-present) was the first chief to be reappointed since Milwaukee's first chief, Walter Beck (1855-1861, 1863-1878, 1880-1892).[5]

THE REFORM ERA: MILWAUKEE AT THE LEADING EDGE OF AMERICAN POLICING

With the passage of the late nineteenth-early twentieth century legislation empowering chiefs, Milwaukee became a model for the Reform (or professional) movement in American policing.[6] Implementation of these laws not only established the long sought after police chief tenure and autonomy, but also employment standards, examinations to determine the fitness for appointment to the police department, and the terms under which chiefs could be dismissed. So armed, Chief Janssen moved throughout his career to "professionalize" policing through implementation of training, command and control

5   By national standards an average tenure of five years isn't too bad. Although exact figures are not available, conventional wisdom has it that chiefs of police in the U.S. don't last too long—probably on the average not more than two-three years. By Milwaukee standards, however, five years is a high turnover rate, especially since the terms under which chiefs left were troublesome: Ziarnik quitting out of frustration with the Common Council; Arreola and Jones wanting reappointment; and Hegerty indicating almost a year before her first term ended, that she would not seek reappointment.

6   We must be clear about what is meant by "professional" in policing. In general when we think of professionals, we think of workers who have had lengthy college and professional school training, deal with matters of great concern, have an established body of knowledge and skills, and enjoy high social status—e.g., physicians, professors, and lawyers. The professionalization movement in policing contrasts with these general conceptions. In policing, professionalization came to mean bureaucratization, civil service, centralized command-and-control, pre- and in-service training, and tenure for police chiefs.

measures, and close supervison. Consequently, as sociologist Sidney L. Harring has noted: "Milwaukee's chief John Janssen might well be called America's first professional police chief."[7] When newly elected socialist Mayor Emil Seidel demanded in 1910 that Janssen resign, Janssen publicly told the mayor to "go to hell" and continued in office until 1921, outlasting Seidel by nine years.[8]

Janssen's successor, Jacob Laubenheimer, is generally credited with creating the organizational characteristics that first led to national recognition of the department. As historian John Gurda explains: "A non-partisan, working with Socialist mayor Dan Hoan, Laubenheimer expanded the force, opened a training academy, initiated radio dispatching, and made his department a model of honesty and efficiency."[9] So widespread was the view that Milwaukee had a unique and "professional" department that the 1931 Wickersham Commission report (the first of two national commissions that studied police in the United States) singled it out for special praise:

> Milwaukee is often cited as a city free from crime or where the criminal is speedily detected, arrested, and promptly tried and sent on his way to serve time. No other city has such a record. The citizens there lay it to the fact that the city has had only had only two chiefs of police in 46 years and no control over the chief is even attempted by the politicians since the effort was made many years ago to remove a chief who claimed the right to act independently, freed from the dictation of politicians.[10]

Influential local groups shared this perception. A study of the MPD conducted in 1938 by the Citizens' Bureau of Milwaukee left no doubt, beginning its report with: "The Citizens' Bureau of Milwaukee takes pride and pleasure in submitting this survey of the *excellence of*

---

7   Sidney L. Harring, "The Police Institution as a Class Question: Milwaukee Socialists and the Police, 1900-1915," *Science and Society* (1982): 202-203.

8   McCarthy, "Harold Breier: Imperious, Old-Fashioned," 28.

9   John Gurda, *Cream City Chronicles: Stories of Milwaukee's Past* (Madison: Wisconsin Historical Society Press, 2007), 211.

10   "Wickersham Report on Police," The National Commission on Law Observance and Enforcement Report No. 14, *The American Journal of Police Science* 2, no. 4 (Jul.-Aug. 1931): 337-348.

Milwaukee's Police Department (emphasis added)."[11] The Bureau credited "Five Fortunate Characteristics" with contributing to this excellence: Milwaukee's law abiding population; the city's manageable area/size that lent itself to foot and motor patrol; the tenure of chiefs;[12] the cooperation of courts; and the maintenance of sufficient funding despite the Great Depression.[13] Finally, historian Samuel Walker describes the leading role that the Milwaukee Police Department played in American policing's professionalization movement:

> Milwaukee's reputation for good government and professional police administration went as far back as the end of the nineteenth century....
>
> The special strengths of the Milwaukee Police Department lay in the area of nonpartisan administration and personnel practices....
>
> Milwaukee also led the way by the 1930s in personnel practices. A police academy was introduced in 1923 with 1 1/2 hours of training per week for all members of the force....[14]

Milwaukee's national preeminence in policing continued until well after World War II. Representatives of other American police departments and police from other countries regularly visited Milwaukee to observe the MPD. One of the department's most noteworthy achievements was its leadership in race relations during and immediately after World War II. After the Detroit race riot of 1943 in which forty-three people were killed, and the Zoot Suit riots between Latino youths and white soldiers in Los Angeles and the Harlem riot after an African American soldier was killed by a police officer the same year, Milwaukee's Chief Joseph Kluchesky (1936-1945)[15] led a select group

---

11   Foreword, Report on Policing (unpub. report, Citizen's Bureau of Milwaukee, September, 1938).

12   The report noted that over the fifty years prior to the study Milwaukee had three chiefs, Chicago twenty-one, Buffalo fourteen, and Detroit sixteen.

13   Citizen's Bureau of Milwaukee, 3-4.

14   Samuel Walker, *A Critical History of Police Reform* (Lexington, MA: Lexington Books, 1977), 164-165.

15   It is worth noting that Chief Kluchesky was only Milwaukee's third police chief in the twentieth century. Chief Janssen was succeeded by Chief Jacob Laubenheimer who remained in office until 1936.

of police drawn from across the country in developing what came to be known as community relations programs. The programs grew out of the belief that antagonism between police and African Americans had contributed both to causes of the riots themselves and to injustices by police in their handling of the riots.[16] While not a popular movement in policing at this time—most chiefs and the International Association of Chiefs of Police (IACP) largely ignored it—community relations programs nonetheless represented an early acknowledgment of the serious challenge that race would present to police departments until well into the twenty-first century.

The community relations movement contained three basic elements: race relations training for police recruits, formal contact between police and African American leaders and the recruitment of black officers, and the development of prescribed techniques for handling disorders.[17] Samuel Walker notes the central role of Chief Kluchesky and the MPD:

> Among police chiefs Joseph Kluchesky quickly emerged as the leading advocate of police-community relations. He initiated a race relations training program in Milwaukee in 1944, wrote a short training manual that many other departments borrowed, lectured to the 1945 IACP [International Association of Chiefs of Police] convention on the race problem, and served as a consultant and instructor for race relations programs in Cleveland, Minneapolis, Youngstown and Dayton. Kluchesky already enjoyed a national reputation as chief of one of the most professional police departments in the country.[18]

While less known, chiefs John Polcyn (1945-1957) and Howard Johnson (1957-1964) continued in the progressive traditions of their predecessors. Both supported and participated in the classic American Bar Foundation Survey (referred to below) during the 1950s when research was unheard of in policing. Unfortunately, Chief Johnson's administration was tainted and probably ended by corruption. A

---

16   See, Samuel E. Walker, "The Origins of the Police-Community Relations Movement: The 1940s," *Criminal Justice History: An International Journal* 1 (New York: John Jay Press, 1980): 225-246, for a detailed history of police community relations during this era.

17   Samuel Walker, *A Critical History of Police Reform*, 234.

18   Samuel Walker, "Origins of the Police-Community Relations Movement," 817.

1962 John Doe investigation discovered widespread misconduct in the MPD's vice and traffic units. Six officers were charged with criminal offenses; thirty-five resigned. Charges involving the Milwaukee Police Department, the Sheriff's department, and at least one suburban police department included bribery, fixing traffic tickets, protecting prostitutes and gambling, and false swearing. [19] Chief Johnson pressed the investigation, and promised swift and aggressive reforms, but retired shortly after the disclosures. At the request of the Fire and Police Commission, he remained chief until a successor could be chosen.[20] Although this corruption was appropriately considered serious, in retrospect a small number of officers were involved and it seemed an aberration from the traditions of policing that Milwaukee had established.

With Milwaukee at the leading edge of American policing during the first half of the twentieth century, police organizations across the country developed a coherent strategy that endured well into the twenty-first century. It embraced the following principles:

  ✦ police derived their authority from the criminal law and their own expertise—not politicians;

  ✦ police business was responding to and investigating serious crimes;

  ✦ police would be organized hierarchically with information flowing up and orders flowing down;

  ✦ law-breaking was clear and easy to recognize; therefore line police work was routine and nondiscretionary;

  ✦ the relationship between police and citizens was best described by the metaphor of the thin blue line—police stand between good and bad citizens, protecting the good and enforcing the law against the bad;

  ✦ primary police tactics included preventive patrol by automobile, rapid response to calls for service, and criminal investigation;

---

19 "John Doe Probe Startles Milwaukee," *Milwaukee Sentinel,* January 7, 1964.

20 Ibid.

    ✦ police performance would be measured by the number of arrests, cases cleared, and response time (the time it takes for police to arrive on the scene once they are contacted).

The parameters of this strategy had been established by O. W. Wilson's 1943 classic *Police Administration*, a text (and its updated editions) that any officer dutifully studied if s/he had any hopes of passing a civil service examination.[21]

    This powerful strategy had much to commend it. It reduced corruption and inappropriate political interference; it improved the administrative capacities of departments; police leaders and line personnel bought into it; and it "made sense" to politicians and the general public. Who really doubted that having police patrol in cars was more efficient than old-fashioned foot patrol or that responding quickly to calls for service would capture the "bad guys" with "smoking guns"? Finally, it recognized the need to develop measures of police effectiveness. Nevertheless the strategy departed markedly from the original Anglo Saxon model of policing. More than anything else, it moved police *away from* crime prevention and *toward* law enforcement, that is, responding to crime after it occurred. This was policing by the 1960s, with Milwaukee a proud world-class police department at the leading edge of the Reform Era. The certainties of the Reform model of policing, however, were sorely challenged during the next decades.

CHALLENGES TO THE REFORM STRATEGY IN POLICING

In many senses urban policing "worked" in the first half of the twentieth century because police operated within and as part of communities and neighborhoods where informal social control provided a foundation for their efforts. By the middle of the century, however, American society was on the threshold of a cultural revolution. Milwaukee itself was entering a period of demographic and economic transition. This era ushered in a series of reforms in government that in fact broke up local communities, displaced residents, and eliminated the social control that had helped keep crime in check. The Reform model of policing that at first thrived in Milwaukee would also be confronted by accumulating research into actual police functioning and effectiveness,

---

21   O. W. Wilson, *Police Administration* (New York: John Wiley & Sons, 1943).

and by the loss of touch of police with citizens in their neighborhoods—especially African Americans. All this took place at the time
that crime began its seemingly inexorable rise.

Destructive Consequences of Urban Policy in Milwaukee

Many problems confronted reform-minded policy makers during
the post World War II period: lack of adequate housing, unmanageable
automobile traffic, abuse of psychiatric patients, injustice to juveniles,
school segregation, and others. Reformers responded with programs
of urban renewal, expressway construction, busing to end school segregation, juvenile court reform, decriminalization of minor offenses,
deinstitutionalization of the emotionally disturbed, and, in the name
of efficiency, centralization of local government services (e.g., courts,
police, and public works). Such efforts often served inadvertently to
weaken institutions of socialization and social control, especially families, schools, and neighborhoods. When traditional mechanisms of
social control were diminished, nothing took their place. Policing is a
good example of the consequences of centralization. The central tenets
of the Reform Movement in policing that developed during the 1920s
but extended into the mid-twentieth century, included centralized
control and operations. The associated tactics called for removing police from city streets and neighborhoods and putting them in cars, responding to crimes already committed. The outcomes were a reduced
police presence in neighborhoods and many negative consequences
that are explored more fully below.

As in many American cities during the 1950s and 1960s, Milwaukee's
growing problems arose from local policy decisions and demographic
changes that intersected with an evolving national culture and policies. One local feature clearly impacting Milwaukee was an unmis-
takable antagonism towards and fear of African Americans that ran
through many areas of public policy, especially housing and education.
Racism's influence on the growth and development of the Milwaukee
Police Department too was profound and undeniable. Chapter Three
below examines the experience of African Americans in Milwaukee
and their interactions with the police department in greater detail;
here, we confine the discussion to looking briefly at how some reform
policies impacted the Sixth Ward, an area in which many African
Americans initially settled and one that would become later one of
Milwaukee's most troubled high crime areas.

Located on the near north side of downtown Milwaukee and to the west of the Milwaukee River, the Sixth Ward was populated largely by Germans, and later Jews and Greeks, throughout most of the late nineteenth and first decades of the twentieth centuries. Known variably as the "inner city north" or "Kilbourntown" (after Byron Kilbourn, an early settler and developer and a real rascal)[22] and one of Milwaukee's oldest neighborhoods, it also served as the entry point for later arriving African Americans, with some areas stigmatized as "Nigger Alley" or "Black Bottom."[23] By around 1940, African Americans numbered about 8,800, and made up less than 2 percent of Milwaukee's population.[24] Virtually all lived within one square mile of Kilbourntown with "Bronzeville"—the neighborhood's shopping and entertainment center—at its core.[25] Small though the black community was at first, its population grew steadily, drawn by wartime jobs in Milwaukee's industrial plants. By 1950 the number had increased to 21,772 (3.4 percent of the city's population); by 1960, 61,458 (8.4 percent); and by 1970, 105,088 (14.7 percent).[26]

The surge of black in-migration during the 1940s and 1950s coincided with a severe housing shortage in Milwaukee. This scarcity had its origins during World War I, but as former Milwaukee Mayor Frank Zeidler noted, the subsequent Great Depression and World War II exacerbated the problem:

> In the period from the Great Depression beginning in 1929 to 1946, there was a severe shortage of housing accommodations in the city.
>
> There was little building during the Depression period, which lasted until 1939, after which war orders revived business. Then there was even less building except for temporary shelter during the war. As a result, in the late 1940's an issue arose of providing

---

22   John Gurda, *The Making of Milwaukee* (Milwaukee, WI: Milwaukee County Historical Society, 1999), 32-33.

23   John McCarthy, "Dreaming of A Decentralized Metropolis: City Planning in Socialist Milwaukee," *Michigan Historical Review* 32, no. 1 (Spring 2006): 42.

24   Julie Boatright Wilson, "Milwaukee: Industrial Metropolis on the Lake" (unpublished monograph, Harvard University, April 1955), 72.

25   Ibid., 74.

26   Ibid., 76.

necessary housing for returning war veterans for meeting the general housing shortage.[27]

Moreover, from as far back as the first decades of the twentieth-century, reformers were concerned about the extent of what they saw as Milwaukee's crowded housing conditions, deteriorated housing stock, and slums. For reformers (primarily socialists in the Progressive tradition), Milwaukee's housing problems, while not as obvious as in New York or Chicago tenements, nonetheless were serious and placed it among the most congested of cities for its size.[28] According to these reformers crowded housing conditions led to disease, moral turpitude and social corruption.[29]

Three housing innovations gave rise to their claims: "Polish flats," "German duplexes," and "alley housing." Polish flats developed primarily to the south of Milwaukee's downtown, and represented industrious attempts on the part of Polish immigrants both to own their own homes and improve economically. Former Milwaukee Mayor John Norquist describes them and their function:

> To the Polish immigrants, home ownership was not the result of success, but a means to success... The Polish flat was a modest three- or four-room cottage built with the first money these immigrants could save in their new land. As the mortgage was paid off, the owner of the cottage typically would raise it on posts four or five feet high in order to construct a semibasement living space, with a separate entrance, below. Sometimes this space was occupied by newly arrived, income-earning members of the owner's family; sometimes it was let to boarders. As soon as additional income allowed, the timber beams of the basement were replaced with brick walls.[30]

---

27   Frank Zeidler, "Some Conditions in Milwaukee at the Time of *Brown v. Board of Education,*" *Marquette Law Review* 89 (2005): 75.

28   John McCarthy, "Dreaming of a Decentralized Metropolis," 40-41.

29   Milwaukee had three socialist mayors during the period 1910 to 1960—Emil Seidel (1910-1912), Daniel Hoan (1916-1940), and Frank Zeidler (1948-1960—for thirty-eight out of fifty years. See Paul Boyer, *Urban Masses and Moral Order in America: 1820-1920* (Cambridge: Harvard University Press, 1978), 234-235, for a fascinating discussion of these issues.

30   John O. Norquist, *The Wealth of Cities: Revitalizing the Centers of American Life* (Cambridge, MA: Basic Books, 1998), 101-102.

The Germans who settled in Milwaukee on the near north side, west of the Milwaukee River, generally came from wealthier backgrounds and possessed more urban and artisan skills than most other nineteenth century immigrants. Nonetheless they too developed unique housing styles: the two-story flat in which the owner lived either up or downstairs and rented the other story. Finally, throughout the city many owners of relatively small lots built "alley houses" on the back of their lots, either to rent or to house immigrant relatives.[31]

The extent to which these residential areas actually constituted threats to health and morality so that as they aged they required strong governmental action is arguable. Nathan Glazer, for example, has argued that New York's tenement housing stock provided quite adequate shelter and what remains of it in New York City is now more desirable housing than public developments that replaced them. Glazer argues that the problem was *overcrowding*—not dilapidation.[32] Regardless, reformers were convinced that the city would be better off without some of these traditional neighborhoods with their "sub-standard" housing stock. Efforts to eliminate many such areas constituted a core component of urban renewal in Milwaukee.

Events reached a critical point by the 1960s and 1970s: Milwaukee was in the midst of a demographic and economic transformation. The city's population peaked in 1960 at 741,324, but declined to 717,099 by 1970. Black immigration continued to climb. Suburbanization increased—annexations by the city dropped from 260 (covering sixteen square miles) during 1950-1959 to fifteen (.05 square miles) during 1960-1969—as a result of changed state laws.[33] Meanwhile, eight new suburbs incorporated as separate entities. At the same time Milwaukee's share of the SMSA (Standard Metropolitan Statistical Area)[34] firms declined from 1947 to 1972: in manufacturing from 76 percent to 47 percent, in service from 76 percent to 51 percent, in

31   Such approaches to housing were not unusual but took particular forms depending on location: Boston had triplexes; other cities, especially in the South had one-story shotgun houses; Baltimore and Philadelphia had two-story row houses.

32   Cited in Howard Husock, "Nathan Glazer's Warning," *City Journal* (Summer 2011): 87.

33   Wilson, 45.

34   Milwaukee's SMSA includes Milwaukee, Ozaukee, Racine, Washington, and Waukesha Counties.

wholesale from 89 percent to 48 percent, and in retail from 66 percent to 49 percent.[35] Overall then, Milwaukee's population was declining; geographical expansion was blocked; African Americans were moving into Milwaukee in increasing numbers; and jobs were moving out of the city to the suburbs and outlying areas. Harvard University's Julie Wilson summarizes:

> The Milwaukee region continued growing throughout the 1940s, 1950s, and 1960s, supported by a strong manufacturing base. However, by 1970, the city of Milwaukee was losing populations and jobs at a rapid rate... The downtown was being revitalized, but blacks were still trapped in low-skill, low-pay jobs, had limited access to housing, and received poorer quality services than their white counterparts. The city was poised for enormous political confrontations over the subsequent two decades.[36]

Regardless of their intentions policy-makers of the time adopted development practices that ultimately destroyed many lower class neighborhoods in Milwaukee and exacerbated racial discord. For example, the decision to demolish Bronzeville, the core commercial African American area in the Sixth Ward, to build an expressway led to a cascade of debilitating forces.[37] When their homes were demolished, African Americans in Bronzeville scrambled to find residences in adjacent, similar high-density neighborhoods largely to the north and northwest. Redlining limited displaced families from purchasing homes. At the same time block busting was set in motion: real estate agents frightened whites in surrounding areas into selling their homes at depressed prices because African Americans would be moving in from adjacent redevelopment neighborhoods.[38] As former Mayor Zeidler notes: "Whites felt they had lost property value and were being forced out, and African Americans felt they were being charged excessively for property."[39] Both outcomes arose from circumstances certain to create antagonism among races. The lag between planning and execution created further problems. Again, Julie Wilson explains: "Because homes and businesses in this area were scheduled to be de-

35   Wilson, 76-79.

36   Ibid., 101

37   Zeidler, 76.

38   Ibid, 78-79.

39   Ibid, 78.

molished, homes were not repaired. Many houses stood vacant and vandalized; fires were commonplace."[40] Useful and affordable housing stock was not replaced: between 1960 and 1970, 7,337 houses were destroyed in predominately African American neighborhoods and replaced by only 1,198 units, of which 254 were for low income residents.[41]

If land redevelopment wreaked havoc through physical dislocation, this upheaval also resulted in the loss of residents—black and white alike—from familiar neighborhoods, breaking up social, economic, and political networks. These networks had provided a source of structure, norms, and social control within neighborhoods that was soon missing. Furthermore, the neighborhoods into which displaced residents moved were not necessarily settings conducive to maintaining such social control. For example, many whites moved out of their neighborhoods into other residential areas (both urban and suburban) that were shaped by "rigid zoning ordinances that promoted the detached, single-family home." Such zoning, with the larger lots it mandated, was intended to "bring urban dwellers closer to the regenerative powers of nature and produce a better life for citizens of the city."[42] Yet single-purpose zoning in fact eliminated the corner grocery store, bakery, and tavern by concentrating them on main commercial arteries and eliminating them from residential areas. With them went the watchful eyes of neighborhood shopkeepers, and a steady flow of pedestrians and customers on the streets. It was, as John McCarthy points out, "a means to segregate cities functionally and economically."[43]

Jane Jacobs in her 1962 classic *The Death and Life of Great American Cities* anticipated the negative social consequences that would result from the loss of mixed-use neighborhoods. She was right: when "ownership" of public places by citizens themselves declined in Milwaukee, as in many other American cities, so too did the social control it brought to urban settings.[44]

---

40   Wilson, 93-94.

41   Ibid.

42   McCarthy, "Dreaming of a Decentralized Metropolis," 35.

43   Ibid., 37.

44   Jane Jacobs, *The Death and Life of Great American Cities* (New York: Vintage Books, 1961). Other illustrations of such urban displacement could be given both within Milwaukee and other cities. Milwaukee's

A Cultural and Legal Revolution: Individual Rights and the Loss of Social Control

It was not land redevelopment and highway construction alone that weakened social control over public spaces. Cultural and legal changes taking place on the national scene only added to the growing sense of mayhem on city streets. Although not entirely apparent at the time, by the 1960s a cultural revolution had begun that would transform American culture from top to bottom. The groundwork for some of the transformations was laid during the 1950s. Over the next few decades these groundbreaking events and changes were both broad and profound.

For me this cultural upheaval manifested itself in terms of three trends or categories each characterized by significant milestones, of which only a few are mentioned here. First, a number of crucial legal decisions, combined with changes in thinking about crime, fundamentally altered the landscape of criminal justice. Urban crime and crime control moved front and center in American politics, as was evident in the 1964 presidential election when Republican candidate Barry Goldwater made urban crime a major political issue in his race against President Lyndon Johnson. Furthermore, a series of Supreme Court decisions placed limits and requirements on police actions. In 1961,

---

Historic Third Ward (HTW), now restored decades later as a vibrant mixed-use urban area, was also a community destroyed both by urban renewal and highway construction. An area of the city originally settled by Irish, the HTW was destroyed twice: first, by a massive fire that demolished over 400 buildings during the 1890s, after which it was settled by the first generation of Italians to move into the area; second, by urban renewal and expressway construction during the 1960s. (I recall one of my professors at UW-Milwaukee's School of Social Work, who had formerly been an important player in developing housing and redevelopment policy, justifying the forced displacement of the Italian community in HTW on the basis of America's "melting pot." As he lectured, "It was time for the Italians to integrate into Milwaukee's culture.") The impact of such policies on the HTW were so great that those few residents of the area not displaced had to fight "city hall" during the 1960s and 1970s to keep officials from turning what remained of the area into a "red light" district. Even now, the downtown freeway and interchange create, as Ron San Fellipo who heads the HTW's business improvement district (BID) puts it, a "great divide" between a rejuvenated downtown and the HTW. Ron San Fellipo interview by George Kelling, August 5, 2011.

Mapp v. Ohio established that the exclusionary rule, prohibiting illegal searches and seizures, was applicable in state courts. The Miranda decision followed in 1966 requiring police to inform defendants of their right to counsel. And in 1967, the Gault decision accorded juveniles virtually the same rights as adults when accused of crimes.[45]

Second, turmoil in politics and culture occurred, with often volatile assertions of rights taking place in new areas and by groups that had not previously been powerful—students, poor people, environmentalists, anti-war protestors. In 1962, Rachel Carson's *The Silent Spring* inaugurated the environmental movement. Four years later, the National Welfare Rights Organization sought to legitimize welfare as a citizen right and pushed for a guaranteed annual income as an alternative to then-current welfare policies. This was also an era in which youth declared their presence and their intent to effect change, often by questioning authority and the establishment. The appearance of the Beatles on The Ed Sullivan Show in 1964 symbolized the establishment of youth culture; the same year the Free Speech Movement, with its demand by students for rights to engage in political activity on campus, began in Berkeley, California. The Vietnam war also became an issue beginning in 1964, transitioning into a ground war phase when troops were sent to Vietnam to protect air bases. Many of these movements played out on streets and in public places where police, who could not remain aloof, became targets, their vulnerabilities exposed. This was clearly evident in 1967 when the Dow Chemical demonstrations in Madison, Wisconsin led to a rebellion against police handling of demonstrators.

Finally, a questioning of traditionally accepted gender roles and sexual preferences, along with the civil rights movement and its assertion of the rights of minorities, led to what many perceived to be a revolt against authority. In 1959 *Lady Chatterley's Lover* by D. H. Lawrence was published in the United States, symbolizing the development of new standards in literature and sexual behavior. Betty Friedan's *The Feminine Mystique* in 1963 appeared, a founding pillar of the women's rights revolution. And the Stonewall (gay pride) riots in New York City in 1969 began the gay rights movement. At the same time fundamental changes involving race in America were already underway.

---

45   Mapp v. Ohio, 367 U.S. 643, 81 S. Ct. 1684, 6 L.Ed. 2d 1081 (1961);
      Miranda v. Arizona, 384 U.S. 436, 86 S.Ct. 1602, 16 L.Ed. 2d 694 (1966);
      In re Gault, 387 U.S. 1, 87 S.Ct. 1428, 18 L.Ed. 2d 527 (1967).

The 1954 Brown v. Board of Education decision banned school segregation and in 1964 the Civil Rights Act outlawed discrimination in public spaces, schools and employment.[46] Then during 1964-1965, riots occurred in Harlem and Rochester, Jersey City and Elizabeth, New Jersey, Los Angeles (Watts), and other locations, representing the African American rebellion against racial discrimination. Marches in southern states were another part of this story: in 1965 the Selma to Montgomery marches documented police abuse of demonstrators that was captured for television audiences. Milwaukee's own 1967 riot brought home the African American revolt against police.

Certainly other important political and cultural happenings during this time could be identified. Together they ushered in an era of rapid social change, the scope of which cannot be exaggerated. Many issues associated with the events and trends mentioned above have been resolved; others remain contentious and divisive even today. Regardless, during the 1960s they tested police on a daily basis and were often played out in public arenas where police were on the front lines. For example, across the country deinstitutionalization put severely mentally disturbed persons on the streets without providing resources for local care. Decriminalization of minor offenses such as drunkenness increased social disorder.[47] Bussing to end school segregation reduced oversight of children walking to local schools and sent them far out of their own familiar neighborhoods. At the same time legal and administrative challenges to the authority of principals and teachers weakened their controls within schools.[48] All of this was part of a broad cultural movement emphasizing the rights of individuals over their responsibilities, a movement that lost sight of the value of communities themselves and the fact that communities could be victimized, and that challenged virtually all forms of traditional authority.[49]

46   Brown v. Board of Education of Topeka, 398 U.S. 886, 75 S.Ct. 210 (1954); The Civil Rights Act of 1964 (Pub.L. 88–352, 78 Stat. 241, enacted July 2, 1964).

47   David E. Aaronson, C. Thomas Dienes, and Michael C. Musheno, "Changing the Public Drunkenness Laws: The Impact of Decriminalization," *Law & Society Review* 12 (1977): 405.

48   Kay S. Hymowitz, "Who Killed School Discipline?" *City Journal* (Spring 2000).

49   For extensive discussion of these issues, see Mary Ann Glendon, *Rights Talk: The Impoverishment of Political Discourse* (New York: Free Press,

Even the authority of parents over their children was weakened. One personal example: during the 1980s, I participated in an Executive Session on Juvenile Justice at Harvard University's Kennedy School of Government in which regular meetings over a several-year period brought together practitioners, policy makers, academics, and politicians to discuss trends and the state of public policy related to juvenile justice. I had not worked in juvenile justice since around 1965 but was aware that dramatic changes had taken place—the most significant resulting from the Supreme Court's 1967 Gault decision ruling that juveniles be afforded the same due process rights as adults. Gault overturned the traditional view that such rights did not apply to juveniles because the juvenile court itself was to act as surrogate parent in the best interests of the child. After Gault the juvenile court became an adversarial arena in the treatment of juvenile delinquents.[50]

With my professional interests focused on police since the early 1970s, I was interested in how juvenile courts actually functioned in the 1980s compared with how they had functioned earlier. As part of my contribution to the Session I visited two jurisdictions in which I had earlier worked: Hennepin County (Minneapolis), Minnesota, and Milwaukee County, Wisconsin. What struck me most vividly was how little authority I would have as a parent in this new scheme if my child stole a car at age thirteen. Years ago I would have insisted that he acknowledge his guilt and accept the consequences. In this new world my child and his attorney could decide together to plead him innocent: it was their decision; I would have no standing in the court; and if I refused to pay for an attorney, the court would appoint one. In other words in the name of protecting my child from potential abuse by juvenile justice agencies, my parental authority to determine the best interests for him had been taken away. I am not arguing here that abuses did not occur in juvenile justice during the pre-Gault era, nor do I seek to debate the relative merits of "in the interest of" or "due process" models of juvenile justice. My point is that to uphold one set of values—protecting juveniles from abuse—a juvenile justice system evolved that ignored another set of values. The authority that parents

1991), and Lawrence M. Friedman, *The Republic of Choice: Law, Authority, and Culture* (Cambridge: Harvard University Press, 1990).

50   For a thorough discussion of these issues, see Gary S. Katzmann, ed., *Securing Our Children's Future: New Approaches to Juvenile Justice and Youth Violence* (Washington, D.C.: Brookings Institution Press, 2002).

had over their children became one more institution, the family, weak-ened by well-intentioned social action.

Certainly much was gained during the era of the 1960s and 1970s. Today we enjoy the benefits achieved from the drive to obtain civ-il rights for minorities and women; other examples of just outcomes could be given. Still other aspects of these social changes appear linked, in hindsight, to unanticipated consequences. The significant increase in urban crime may well have been one—and perhaps should not have been surprising.

The Increase in Crime

For those inclined to commit crimes, the erosion in social control that unwittingly arose from new social policies presented a range of new opportunities to engage in illegal behavior. Gone were the neigh-borhood networks that warned parents of their children's misbehav-ior. Gone were the watchful eyes of parents as their children walked to school. Gone was the ownership that neighborhood merchants exer-cised over the public spaces that led to their stores. And so on. While none of these changes may have mattered that much individually, the across-the-board decline in social control in neighborhoods, schools, and even families, and the increasing public disorder created by the presence of the mentally ill and petty offenders was just too stimulat-ing for youthful predators.

The vast majority of young people adjusted to these changes with relatively few problems. They went to school, respected their parents and adults, perhaps experimented with some misbehavior, but stayed within normal bounds. For a small percentage, however, these changes opened a Pandora's box of violence, robbery, theft, and mayhem—not to mention myriad minor offenses. We have known since 1972 that six percent of young people who offend carry out fifty percent of crimes committed.[51] The study of youth born in 1945 that produced these findings was replicated in 1985 with a cohort of youth born in 1958.[52] The second study's findings were instructive: the percentage of youth who accounted for a large portion of crimes remained at six percent;

51   Marvin Wolfgang, Robert Figlio, and Thorsten Sellin, *Delinquency in a Birth Cohort* (Chicago: University of Chicago Press, 1972).

52   Paul Tracy, Marvin Wolfgang, and Robert Figlio, *Delinquency in Two Birth Cohorts* (Washington, D.C.: Office of Juvenile Justice and Delinquency Prevention, 1985).

however, *both the number and seriousness of their offenses increased.* In other words, a small percentage of youth, the "six percenters" as they are known, were vulnerable to the loosening of controls that occurred during the 1960s and '70s. Although new formal studies are not readily available today, police and residents in most neighborhoods can tell you who the serious troublemakers are, and will confirm their relatively small number as well as the enormous consequences of their activities for the area.

What do we know of Milwaukee's crime increase during the 1960s and beyond in light of the changes we considered above? As Figure 1 below indicates, crime levels in Milwaukee had remained constant from the 1940s through 1955, when virtually all crimes began a steep increase with larceny, burglary, and auto theft leading the way.[53] More ominously, although robbery, a crime of violence or threatened violence, got off to a slow start, by 1980 it was climbing steeply. Once set in motion, the rise in crime proved difficult to stem.

Since Milwaukee's population dropped between 1960 and 1990 by over 100,000, from 741,324 to 628, 088, the crime problem was even worse than the figure would suggest.[54]

One further consequence that continued to hinder police was that even when crime did begin to fall after 2000, citizens were loath to believe it. In Milwaukee, although violent crime dropped by 23 percent and property crime by 18.5 percent between 2007 and 2010, one poll indicated that only 16 percent believed crime had declined, while 33 percent believed it had increased.[55] Several interpretations

---

53   Readers should exercise caution in reading this table. While I am comfortable that it reflects the overall trends, the numbers for specific crimes for specific years should be considered approximations. These data were taken from MPD annual reports, and they may or may not be accurate depending on the year, recording policy, unfounded crimes, and other vagaries that can affect police department recording practices over time. Milwaukee Police Department Annual Reports, 1940, 1945, 1950, 1955, 1960, 1965, 1970, 1975, 1980, 1985, 1990.

54   Population history of Milwaukee from 1850-1990, accessed October 17, 2014, http://www.physics.bu.edu/~redner/projects/population/cities/milwaukee.html.

55   Stacey Vogel Davis, "Public Wrongly Perceives Crime on Rise, Poll Finds," *Business Journal,* April 1, 2011, p. A10, reporting on a survey conducted by the University of Wisconsin-Milwaukee, *Business Journal* and the Public Policy Forum.

are possible for these findings: one is that citizen lack of trust and confidence in the police department extended for so long that it may have undermined police credibility. Another possible explanation may be that while serious crime declined, the level of urban decay and minor crimes continued to send a message to citizens that things were out of control. Finally issues such as high levels of unemployment could have contributed to a sense that nothing had really changed. The fact is that we do not know exactly what accounts for citizen perceptions of crime that did not exactly track actual crime reductions in these areas.

Even though I argue here that the crime surge over the last forty years was intrinsically linked to social policy and cultural changes, police in Milwaukee were not impotent bystanders. For too long they remained bound to an ineffective strategy that prevented them both from returning to what had worked in an earlier era and from exploring promising changes that police in other American cities were developing.

Challenges to Policing's Conventional Wisdom

Despite the momentous challenges facing them, police entered the 1960s confident that they had in place an overall strategy that was both effective in crime control and efficient, that most police corruption and politics had been eliminated from policing, and that, if not truly professional in the classic sense of the term, police were at least on the path to professionalism. For most police, all the policing questions had been asked and all the answers given. Yet during the 1960s two ideas emerged to upset accepted thinking about police and their self-confidence.

The first challenge to conventional wisdom was the research finding that police work was not simple and routine. This challenge grew out of observational research of police conducted by social scientists such as James Q. Wilson,[56] Egon Bittner[57] and others, and the American Bar Foundation. This new evidence convincingly portrayed police activities as ranging far beyond mere law enforcement. These findings belied O. W. Wilson's (the dominant mid twentieth-century police

56   James Q. Wilson, *Varieties of Police Behavior: The Management of Law and Order in Eight Communities* (Cambridge, Harvard University Press, 1968).

57   Egon Bittner, "Police on Skid Row: a Study of Peace Keeping," *American Sociological Review* 32 (1967): 600-715.

	1940	1945	1950	1955	1960	1965	1970	1975	1980	1985	1990
Criminal Homicide											
Murder & Non Negligent	11	13	10	14	15	36	50	69	74	73	165
Rape	35	44	36	61	32	39	93	146	213	426	598
Robbery	57	90	82	93	157	257	649	1968	1796	2271	4472
Agg. Assault	53	102	149	257	480	2665	3051	1020	1227	1519	1513
Burglary	592	887	673	786	1738	3033	4303	7685	9638	7781	9331
Larceny											
Over $50	305	600	1122	1386	2622	4538	9355	22813	24726	27151	29635
Auto Theft	560	1009	934	957	2052	4242	5018	4816	3772	4615	13336

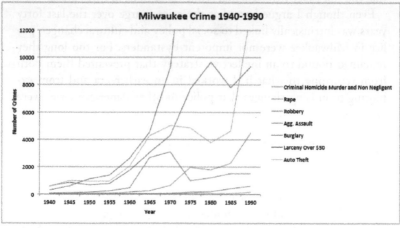

Figure 1
Milwaukee Crime Data, 1940-1990

theorist) analogy that police officers' work was akin to typists' rote copying of a manuscript.[58] In reality, the problems with which police deal are complex and police use extensive discretion to manage them. The full implications of the findings regarding complexity and discretion took decades to work through, and in many cases are not fully understood even now.

The second idea, that American criminal justice was riddled with racism, resulted in calls for immediate action. President Lyndon Johnson's Commission on Law Enforcement and the Administration of Justice emphasized the problems of racism in its 1967 report, *The Challenge of Crime in a Free Society*. American criminal justice agencies, reflecting American culture, were infused with racism—in the

---

58   O.W. Wilson, "Basic Police Policies," *The Police Chief* (November 1956): 28-29.

case of police, both in their tactics and their administrative practices (such as hiring and promotions). The impact of racism was not only unfairness and injustice; it substantially interfered with the ability of police to deal with neighborhood and community problems, especially in African American communities. Police were not only abusive, but ignored the rights of minorities and disregarded their needs. While this federal report addressed a variety of problems, its findings regarding race had the most immediate impact on policing.[59]

I still recall the excitement those of us interested in criminal justice felt about the ideas emphasized by President Johnson's Commission. The report itself called on police to develop community relations programs and to recruit, hire, and promote African Americans. Efforts to do so became a litmus test for attempts to improve policing. As an assistant professor in the School of Social Work at the University of Wisconsin-Milwaukee (1965-1970), I became interested then in policing and advocated for community relations programs to address the deteriorating relationship between minorities and police. Through these activities I met two seminal figures in the field—University of Wisconsin-Madison Law School Professor Herman Goldstein and Michigan State University School of Criminal Justice Professor Lou Radelet. Goldstein was a principal researcher in the American Bar Foundation study and champion of the ideas of complexity in police work and the ubiquity of discretion. Radelet was a well-known advocate of community relations who worked with the National Institute for Police and Community Relations at Michigan State University and authored several community relations textbooks. Both would influence my later work: Goldstein as one of my professors at the University of Wisconsin-Madison when I worked on my Ph.D. there and for his publications on problem-oriented policing, and Radelet as an early proponent in the movement towards a community orientation in policing and crime prevention.[60]

---

59 President Johnson created the Office of Law Enforcement Assistance (OLEA, 1965-1968) that later was expanded to the Law Enforcement Assistance Administration (LEAA, 1968-1982). LEAA would pump over $8 billion into state and local police and criminal justice agencies. (Although LEAA was disbanded in 1982, the Department of Justice maintains a reduced level of outreach through the Office of Justice Programs.)

60 See, Herman Goldstein, "Improving Policing: A Problem-Oriented Approach," *Crime & Delinquency* (April 1979): 236-243, and Louis A.

On top of these challenges to conventional police views, the results of the first generation of operations research conducted during the 1970s cast further doubt on the overall strategy of police. The results—stunning at the time but now commonly acknowledged—challenged the effectiveness of preventive patrol by automobile, the value of rapid response to calls for service, and the efficacy of criminal investigation (at least as it was conducted at that time). Police randomly riding around in cars appeared to prevent nothing; rapid response to calls for service rarely had a beneficial impact; and criminal investigations as conducted in most departments during the 1970s were found merely to be the primary means by which cases were prepared for court (essentially a secretarial function), based as they were on preliminary investigations previously conducted by patrol officers.[61] In sum, little that police work involved was proving effective in reducing crime.

ENTER HAROLD BREIER

In the midst of cultural turmoil, demographic changes in Milwaukee, new understandings of police functioning, and concern about police racism, Harold Breier was appointed Milwaukee's police chief on March 17, 1964. Breier had joined the MPD in 1940 at the age of twenty-nine. Not unlike many youths at the time, he held several jobs before becoming a police officer: factory timekeeper, electrician's helper, inspector in a paint factory, and temporary deputy sheriff.[62] Three years after his appointment as a police officer he became an acting detective; in 1946, full detective; 1951, detective sergeant; 1954, lieutenant of detectives; 1958, captain of detectives; 1960, deputy inspector of detectives; 1962, inspector of detectives. Finally in 1964, after serving as acting chief for a month, he was appointed chief.

Breier was already a colorful character when appointed Milwaukee Chief of Police. While inspector of detectives he had wanted to be in the action constantly, insisting that he be called out for major crimes regardless of the time of day or night; he earned the department's highest award for arresting a murder suspect after a gun battle; and he

---

Radelet, *The Police and the Community* (Glencoe, IL: Glencoe Press, 1973).

61   For a summary of this research, see Kelling and Coles, *Fixing Broken Windows*, chap. 3.

62   Ronald H. Snyder, "Chief for Life: Harold Breier and His Era" (Ph.D. dissertation, University of Wisconsin-Milwaukee, December 2002), 23.

was open, available to, and favored by, the media: when something exciting happened media reps wanted to talk to the voluble Breier.[63] His views about policing were simple: "We enforce the laws. You take an oath to enforce the ordinances of the state and the city. And that's it."[64]

Breier's First Deal

Less than a week after his inauguration Breier set the tone of his administration. He addressed his officers in three sessions (to accommodate shifts), promising to "set policy for the department" and be its sole spokesperson.[65] But there was more. As historian Ronald H. Snyder recounts, Breier further emphasized his autonomy and how he would use his immunity to protect officers:

> Two weeks after taking office, he announced that an internal investigation of the traffic ticket-fixing scandal, launched by his immediate predecessor, had been halted and that the officers conducting the investigation had returned to their regular duties. The chief said that he would neither reveal disciplinary actions taken against police officers nor cooperate with an Assistant State Attorney General who was investigating police corruption.[66]

For Breier police business was just that: *police* business! He staked out his position from the beginning, in effect striking a deal with his officers. It went something like this: I, and I only, will speak for the MPD. No outsiders speak for the MPD. Any officers who speak to the media will be disciplined. I will protect you and the MPD from any and all external scrutiny: only police can judge police and I can judge you better than anyone else. Those who complain about police are lawbreakers, ultra liberals, communists, or socialists. In turn, you will abide by my requirement for strict adherence to the letter of the law regarding rules and regulations of the MPD—especially having to do with your personal conduct.

In retrospect, one can only surmise how officers decoded Breier's message. Most chiefs of police would be extremely wary of this kind of deal for officers. Certainly most police are going to work properly or, at least, try to. Occasionally even the best of officers will make mistakes

---

63   Ibid., 25–26.

64   McCarthy, "Harold Breier: Imperious, Old-Fashioned," 23.

65   Snyder, 29.

66   Ibid.

and it is entirely reasonable for police executives to try and protect them—not necessarily from all consequences, but at least protect their careers through retraining, supervision, and limited disciplinary action. But police departments, like any large organizations, have their share of incompetents. Assuring them that they would be free from external scrutiny, as Breier arguably did, invited abuse of authority of one kind or another on the part of police and suspicion of cover-ups on the part of citizens. For example, in 1981 an African American citizen falsely accused of rape died while being restrained in a police van. Even before the county medical examiner had determined the cause of death, Breier exonerated the three officers involved, commenting that the lesson to be learned was that citizens should not resist arrest. In doing so, he aggravated an already contentious relationship with the black community and sent a message to officers that they would enjoy immunity when things went awry.[67]

On the other hand, unrestrained by the Fire and Police Commission, civil service, or unions (initially at least), and proclaiming his complete freedom to do so, Breier disciplined officers zealously for any internal organizational misbehavior: for "being untruthful to a superior, having long hair or sideburns, or failing to wear a proper uniform...for engaging in political activity, for not carrying their weapons while off duty, for declaring bankruptcy, and for feigning illness."[68] Breier seemed particularly preoccupied with the sexual activity of officers:

> He ordered officers from the department's Bureau of Internal Affairs and Vice Squad to watch the apartments of unmarried officers suspected of cohabiting with other police officers. As a result of the surveillance, two couples were dismissed.... He suspended a detective lieutenant for three days and reprimanded another for failing to report that a third police officer traveled to a conference with a woman who was not his wife. He fired a male officer for having an extra-marital affair....[69]

Protests by politicians about the costs of such disciplinary processes, concern about the consumption of police time spent spying on other officers, and officer dissatisfaction did little to dissuade Breier. The explicit "deal" he struck with his officers—"I will protect you from any

67   McCarthy, "Harold Breier: Imperious, Old-Fashioned," 31.

68   Synder, 31-32.

69   Ibid.

external review" but "You will abide by my strict enforcement of rules and regulations"—earned Breier the deep respect that was accompanied by fear. Officers might refer to him as a "mean son of a b...h" but he was *their* "mean son of a b...h." He would not only keep the "blue curtain," he would help hang it.

The Other "Deal"

The deal that Breier made with his officers was explicit. He touted it from his earliest days as chief and, with the exception of restraints placed on him by the developing police union, maintained it until he resigned. On the other hand, the deal he made with the community was largely implicit and "rolled out" over time. It looked something like this:

1. I am the sole authority on all Milwaukee police matters.

2. Civilians have no place in policing: this includes individuals (even as civilian employees of the MPD), groups, consultants, and/or, especially, politicians.

3. Police business is inherently secretive: civilians, especially politicians, have no right to access police policies, practices, or rules and regulations.

4. The job of police is to enforce the criminal law; time spent on other activities limits the police ability to fight crime.

5. Since police merely enforce the law, those who do not break the law have nothing to fear from police.

6. Police are the "thin blue line" protecting good citizens from bad.

7. "Black crime" is a threat to white neighborhoods.

8. Critics of police are ultra-liberals, revolutionaries, and/or communists.

9. Milwaukee, because of its police department, is a safe city: ergo the MPD should be left alone to pursue its strategy.

The first thing that should be said about this "deal" is that, for the most part, it was consistent with mainstream American policing at the time (1964). Breier might have driven some of these principles to extremes; other chiefs may not have been as willing as Breier to articulate them; others still might have adhered to them conceptually, but in practice acknowledged that they had to "rise above principle" to maintain satisfactory relations with a mayor or city council. In other words Breier was not alone during the 1960s and into the 1970s: police did claim that "they knew best;" police did see their function solely as crime fighting; police did adhere to the thin blue line metaphor; and although few chiefs would have said it at the time, most did believe that "black crime" threatened white neighborhoods.

The second thing to be said is that regardless of what Chief Breier meant when he talked about "good" and "bad" citizens, a good portion of the general public—both his supporters and his critics—decoded his "good" and "bad" as white and black respectively. Moreover, the small number of blacks (and later Hispanics and women) in the MPD and the almost total lack of blacks in departmental leadership positions added credence to those who believed Breier supported racist policies and practices. A comment made by Breier near the end of his career about busing black crime to white neighborhoods (as a result of busing to achieve school desegregation) did little to disabuse those who held such beliefs.

Tactful or circumspect about his beliefs, Breier was not. In 1966, community relations was for him "hogwash."[70] In 1970 Breier and the director of the police academy rejected higher education for officers with a resounding "no," adding: "There can be no rebuttal to the fact that there are educated fools among us with idealistic, unworkable, and impractical ideas."[71] When presented with some of the research challenging the effectiveness of criminal investigation, he responded "I've read some of the studies and it makes me want to vomit."[72] In 1981, Milwaukee Mayor Maier created a ten-person Special Advisory Monitoring Committee after a young black man, Ernest Lacy, died while in police custody. Breier testified before the Committee but only to make clear that he was "not going to discuss police techniques and procedures with this panel or anyone else," adding that the Committee

---

70   Snyder, 76.

71   Snyder, 39, quoting "Breier Cool to Study Plan for Policemen," *Milwaukee Journal*, May 22, 1968.

72   McCarthy, "Harold Breier: Imperious, Old-Fashioned," 23.

really should be investigating those who were promoting tensions—the Communist Party and the Socialist Workers Party.[73] As for community policing, Breier believed police officers had no time for it. The local police union (the Milwaukee Police Association) wanted the MPD to develop a counseling program for troubled and alcohol-abusing officers. Breier refused, commenting according to then-union president Robert Kliesmet: "Show me a drunken cop and I'll fire the son of a bitch."[74] Breier fought with virtually everyone who threatened his autonomy on policing matters: the Common Council, district attorney, United States Attorney, Fire and Police Commission, community groups, state legislature, academics, clergy, political leaders (e.g., Mayor Maier), the U.S. Department of Justice, and the courts. It is hard to find a group with whom Breier did not fight at one point or another.

Perhaps one of Breier's most outrageous "blurts" came in a meeting with important (ecclesiastical) representatives of the Catholic, Lutheran, Presbyterian, and Jewish faiths. These clergy represented the Greater Milwaukee Conference on Religion and Urban Affairs and met with Breier for the purpose of urging him to take steps to improve the relationship between minorities and police, including developing a community relations program. The chief's response was pure Breier: "I don't tell you how to run your churches. Don't tell me how to run my department. I know what the department needs and what the community needs."[75]

One has to give Breier some credit. A community relations approach was not all that it was held up to be: in many cities, it was nothing more than a public relations effort to sell whatever police were doing. Breier's comments that all his officers were involved in community relations had some truth to it, since all police indeed should be. Likewise, his criticism of academics had some basis: a central theme in criminology at the time was that crime could only be prevented through economic and social change—ergo police could only respond after the fact, a theory largely discredited by the 1990s. The problem was that Breier dismissed the ideas underlying approaches like

73   Snyder, 88.

74   McCarthy, "Harold Breier: Imperious, Old-Fashioned," 24.

75   Ron Elving and Amy Rabideau Silvers, "Breier's Tough Stance Stuns Religious Leaders," *Milwaukee Journal,* February 18, 1982, p. 16.

community relations and higher education: that substantial problems existed between minority communities and police, about which something had to be done; that police could benefit from continued education and research.

Breier did have a substantial following in Milwaukee. For many threatened by the changes going on about them and the erosion of what they saw as public morality, Breier represented the right side in the struggle to maintain decency as well as law and order. Many of us believed he presented the only real political threat to the dynasty that Mayor Henry Maier had established. Many of us also mistakenly believed that Breier would attempt to become mayor. Moreover many Milwaukeeans viewed Breier and his department as the thin blue line protecting them from mayhem.

Still, despite these perceptions, crime increased substantially during Breier's watch. From 1965, the first full year that Breier was chief, to 1984 when he resigned, homicide increased 102 percent, rape 992 percent, robbery 783 percent, aggravated assault 41 percent, burglary 156 percent, larceny 498 percent, and auto theft 8 percent.[76] Milwaukee was not unique: the crime epidemic was a nation-wide phenomenon with which no city had figured out how to deal. And despite Breier's claims that Milwaukee was one of the safest cities in the United States (which it probably was then), it is more likely that Milwaukee's lengthy history of orderliness and law- abiding citizens were the cause rather than policing methods or Breier's law and order rhetoric.

Over time, Breier's rigidity mobilized opposition. To be sure, much of it was cautious: he was a feared political power. Even as the Milwaukee police union, Fire and Police Commission, Common Council, state legislature, and the U.S. Department of Justice moved to curtail his power, most avoided direct attacks on Breier in one fashion or another. Even the legislation that ended lifetime tenure for Milwaukee's police chief exempted Breier from its provisions. In respects, it was the police union that forced the first limitation on the chief's power. Former Milwaukee police union leader Bob Kliesmet is quite explicit:

> It wasn't salary that drove the move towards unionization and militancy, it was Breier's rule enforcement. He was king and if he wanted to get you one way and couldn't, he'd get you in another—and there was no appeal. It was his enforcement of the rules that drove

---

76   These data are based on MPD annual reports for 1965 and 1984.

us from boss-dominated association to a true union. And, finally, in 1973 we got arbitration that gave us the right to appeal.[77]

The repeal of provisions of the 1911 law was achieved in 1984 when the Wisconsin State Legislature empowered Milwaukee's Fire and Police Commission to make departmental rules and regulations, and gave it approval authority over rules and regulations proposed by the chief. Two months later, Chief Breier announced his resignation. It was not just the end of Breier's reign, but the beginning of the end of the Reform Era of policing in Milwaukee.

Yet Chief Breier's legacy established an agenda for the MPD that persisted into the twenty-first century. At its best, this legacy included being a truly corruption-free department, if one defines corruption only as police being "on the take." But it was a troubled legacy in other respects. The department was isolated in the community: it had a bitter relationship with minorities, especially African Americans, and virtually no working relationships with other public or private sector agencies. It was also cut off from the professional development that was taking place across the country in policing. Internally the department's mission had become distorted, even lost: a strong detective culture flourished to the detriment of patrol—the heart of preventive policing; and an empowered militant union emerged. These troubling developments are the focus of the next two chapters. We begin by looking back at issues of race that began before Breier took office, but persisted throughout his administration.

---

77 Robert Kleismet (former MPD officer and PPA head), interview by George Kelling, November 2010.

CHAPTER THREE

POLICING A
RACIALLY DIVIDED CITY

The issue of race has been and remains the most difficult and inflammatory issue that confronts police nationally. The relationship between police and minorities has been shaped by slavery, enforced segregation, police abuse and/or neglect, and African-American crime and victimization. In other words, American police and minorities have a history that has generated mutual distrust and animosity that is inherent in virtually every police/minority interaction, regardless of the intent of either the minority member or the police officer. Milwaukee clearly falls within this pattern.

My introduction to racial issues in Milwaukee began on the Siefert Elementary School playground along 14th Street where I coached during the early 1950s over summer breaks from college.[1] Before then, I had known only a few African Americans in grade school, children of the few families allowed into Parklawn public housing.[2] Other than

---

[1] A "coach" was a summer employee who oversaw the activities on playgrounds.

[2] I remember one racial incident from grade school. The class had one African American, a girl. I recall the names of both the teacher and girl involved, although I will not use them here. It was about fourth grade at Pleasant View School. A student, not the African American girl, asked our teacher to do something, I forget what, but it was something the student could do herself. The teacher responded: "Take care of it yourself, who was your nigger last year"? The teacher paused, sat for a few moments, then pushed her chair back from her desk, walked to the front of the classroom, faced the students and said to C.F. (those were her initials) something like: "C. I apologize. I should not have said what I did. I meant 'slave' but used a bad word to say it. Again, I apologize to you." The teacher then returned to her desk and the class proceeded. That was the end of the incident.

this I had had little contact: blacks were concentrated in a few square blocks in Bronzville during the 1950s when they made up less than four percent (21,000) of Milwaukee's population. Insofar as I recall, my high school, Washington, had no African American students. When I returned to Milwaukee in 1960 after college and a period of work in Minnesota, the African American population had grown to 62,000, comprising just over 8 percent of the city's population. And by 1965 when I returned again after three years away to take up a position at UW-M as an assistant professor concentrating on crime and probation and parole, the racial situation had already heated up, with riots and demonstrations well underway.

Milwaukee's escalating troubles with race were typical of many cities during this era. The 1960s saw an explosion of riots across the United States: in 1964 Harlem and Rochester, New York, Jersey City and Elizabeth, New Jersey, and Philadelphia; in1965 Los Angeles (Watts); in 1966 Benton Harbor, Michigan, and Atlanta, Georgia; in 1967 Tampa, Florida, Buffalo, New York, and Newark and Plainfield, New Jersey, Detroit, and Milwaukee; and, in 1968 Washington D.C., Baltimore, Chicago, Kansas City, Missouri, and Louisville, Kentucky. Over 100 cities experienced riots after the assassination of Martin Luther King in 1968. Many commentators have debated their causes. The Kerner Commission, with which Chief Breier refused to cooperate, linked the conflagrations to long-standing grievances: racism, unemployment, poor housing and education, and inadequate social services.[3] Critics challenged these findings as absolving rioters and blaming society for their actions, and asked why many cities with more racist practices hadn't experienced riots or why riots took place when things were improving relative to the past? What is significant here is not the debate itself, but the fact that nearly every major riot, at least up to Martin Luther King's assassination in 1968, was triggered by an encounter between police and African Americans. It did not matter whether the interaction resulted from a call requesting police services or from action initiated by the police; nor was the nature of the contact between citizens and police an issue. Black citizens simply refused to be policed on then-contemporary terms.

---

3   Karl H. Flaming, "The 1967 Milwaukee Riot: A Historical and Comparative Analysis" (unpublished dissertation, Syracuse University, August 1970), 175.

In spite of the violence and racial dissension that Milwaukee experienced during the 1960s, African Americans helped to create the city of today. Black Milwaukeeans developed a rich cultural heritage that became part of the city's overall character. Black cultural institutions like the Wisconsin Black Historical Society Museum, the City Ballet Theatre, the Ko-Thi Dance Company, and the Hansberry-Sands Theatre Company continue these contributions today. Dealing with racial issues proved to be one of the most important challenges faced by the MPD and those who led it from the middle of the twentieth century forward. Chief Breier utterly failed in this regard. These are the issues we address in this chapter.

AFRICAN AMERICANS IN MILWAUKEE

Bronzeville was the area of earliest settlement by African Americans in Milwaukee. By the 1930s it consisted of an area of approximately fifty square blocks on the near north side. For the most part blacks were restricted to living in this area. By the 1950s, Bronzeville had enlarged considerably, mainly by expanding to the north and west (the Milwaukee River largely blocked expansion to the east and the downtown district precluded expansion to the south).[4] Although poor Bronzeville was in some respects a settled community. Indigenous businesses sprang up, especially along the two main streets of Walnut and Vliet. By 1950 Bronzeville hosted "170 boarding houses, 35 taverns, 27 restaurants, 20 dry cleaners, 15 beauty shops, 12 grocery stores, 11 automobile repair shops, 11 fuel and ice companies, 10 painters and three funeral homes."[5] Bronzeville flourished as a cultural and entertainment center not only for blacks but for whites as well, especially in clubs that played jazz and blues. Clubs like the Metropole, the Flame, Moon Glow and many others were among the few integrated locations in Milwaukee,[6] and drew performers such as Billie Holiday, Duke Ellington, Count Basie, Dizzy Gillespie, and Nat King Cole.[7] Black church congregations thrived in the area, often taking

---

4   Paul H. Geenen, *Milwaukee's Bronzeville: 1900-1950* (San Francisco: Arcadia Publishing, 2006), 7.

5   Ibid., 21.

6   Ibid., 57.

7   Accessed November 21, 2014, http://www.city.milwaukee.gov/ Bronzeville.

over church buildings and synagogues that Germans and Jews had abandoned as they moved out of the area. Many African Americans recall Bronzeville fondly. University of Wisconsin-Milwaukee faculty member Reuben K. Harpole Jr., summarizes:

> Bronzeville was a place where African American families worked hard to make a living and to make a community. The men worked heavy, physical jobs during the day at a factory and then came home and worked the evening hours in their restaurant or in cleaning up their new church building. The women worked long hours as domestics to earn precious savings to start a new business or to make extra money to help their church grow. The children who grew up there went on to live out the lessons of hard work and community, long after the neighborhood itself was gone.[8]

Community activisit Paul H. Geneen recounts:

> Bronzeville watched over the neighborhood children, Chuck Holton remembers. "Your deportment and manners were overseen by the entire community." In a 2006 *Milwaukee Journal* article, former Bronzeville resident Ralph Jefferson remembers smoking a cigarette with a friend on Walnut Street and being scolded by his mother for it by the time he got home.[9]

Anthropologist Ivory Abena Black adds to this picture:

> Bronzeville was more than just a name and more than just a place or time. It was an African American life style. ... The whole community cared for all the children no matter whose child. ... The community elected their [sic] own mayors like Anthony J. Josey, who was Bronzeville's first African American mayor, housed their own doctors, teachers, and engineers. Bronzeville was a city within a city, an African American metropolis which can still be felt today in the hearts and souls of those who lived, experienced, and shared in it.[10]

Even if Bronzeville was not really as benign as portrayed by Harpole, Geneen, and Black, and even if the three engaged in a little historical romanticizing (after all, slum housing did exist, people were poor, overcrowding was a problem), still there is no reason to doubt

8   Reuben K. Harpole, Jr., "Introduction," in Geenen, 9.

9   Geneen, 39.

10   Ivory Abena Black, *Bronzeville a Milwaukee Lifestyle: A Historical Perspective*, revised edition (Milwaukee: The Publishers Group, 2006), 24.

that Bronzeville was a vibrant community with many strengths. But if the lives of African Americans in Milwaukee exhibited many positive characteristics, the broader history of their experiences in the country portrays clear violence, exploitation, and victimization. Unfortunately the structures that permitted the perpetuation of these effects depended upon police involvement from the outset.

THE LEGACY OF RACE AND POLICING IN AMERICA

The troubled relationship between police and African Americans has at least four roots: slavery, the Black Codes, Jim Crow laws, and contemporaneously, the high rate of African Americans who are victimized coupled with the high rate of crimes committed by black youth. These elements of the black experience form a backdrop for policing nationally and they are no less important for Milwaukee itself. The enforcement of American slavery and the fear of slave uprising gave rise to "slave patrols" in Southern states during the early and mid-1740s—argued by some to be the first modern police departments in the US.[11] Armed not merely with legal mandates but whips and guns as well, slave patrols checked on blacks in public spaces, apprehended and punished runaways, interfered with any gatherings of blacks, broke into their homes to search for weapons or contraband, and "punished" African Americans as they saw fit.[12] Following the Civil War, the "Black Codes" were state laws regulating the lives of African Americans well after the 1863 Emancipation Proclamation. These codes lasted into the twentieth century, specifying the kinds of work that freedmen could have and restricting where they could live and their access to property. They contractually bound laborers to specific employers and established vague vagrancy and loitering laws under which, in lieu of fines, African Americans could be "hired out" to white landowners in need of labor.[13]

---

11   Hubert Williams and Patrick V. Murphy, *The Evolving Strategy of Police: A Minority View*, Perspectives on Policing 13 (National Institute of Justice, U.S. Department of Justice, and the Program in Criminal Justice Policy and Management, John F. Kennedy School of Justice, Harvard University, January 1990), 3.

12   Ibid., 4.

13   David M. Oshinsky *Worse than Slavery: Parchman Farm and the Ordeal of Jim Crow* (New York: Free Press, 1997).

Jim Crow laws overlapped the Black Codes and enforced segregation in Southern states until 1965. Supported by the idea of "separate but equal," these laws kept whites and blacks apart in public transportation, restaurants, hotels, schools, and other public places and facilities. The memory and visions of this condition and its bloody end during the 1950s and 1960s remain fresh in many of our minds. This was the early era of television, and conflicts between police and demonstrators were often broadcast into our homes. Many African Americans were active in the conflicts and still more recall those days clearly.

Currently, in the twenty-first century, police activity in response to high levels of victimization of African Americans and the high rate of criminality by black youth has intensified the interaction between police and African Americans in most American cities. Experiences are mixed: racial profiling and overly aggressive policing have often soured the relationship; on the other hand, successful crime prevention by police since the mid-1990s has been welcomed by many African Americans who have long been the most victimized citizen group. Such successes have substantially changed the relationship between African Americans and police for the better in cities such as Los Angeles, New York, and even Milwaukee. Yet the historical legacy remains: overall African Americans in the United States have had unique experiences with police. No other minority groups have endured the centuries long, legally justified control over their lives that African Americans have suffered.

CIVIL RIGHTS IN MILWAUKEE:
KEY PLAYERS, ISSUES, AND EVENTS

The flashpoint for the early civil rights movement in Milwaukee was the February 2, 1958, killing of Daniel Bell, an African American, after he was stopped by two police officers for having a taillight out. The circumstances were ambiguous: Bell ran from police after the stop; a knife was found in his right hand, although Bell was left-handed; witnesses disputed the officers' accounts of what had transpired; and discrepancies developed in the accounts of the two officers. Nonetheless the district attorney and an inquest panel found the killing justifiable.[14] For University of Nebraska Professor Patrick Jones: "The gunshot that killed Daniel Bell was the signal shot for the black freedom movement

---

14　A federal jury ultimately awarded the Bell family $1,700,000.

in Milwaukee." [15] It also established the relationship between the Milwaukee Police Department and the African American community for the rest of the twentieth century.

For the most part, the response of the black community to Bell's death was fragmented. Some black leaders saw the problem as inherent in the migration of rural southerners to urban settings and called for programs to orient and/or rehabilitate black newcomers; others saw the problem as white prejudice and racism and the need to eradicate it; yet others urged that African Americans needed to change circumstances via the ballot box.[16] What was clear was that the African American community was not unified in its understanding of the problems or what steps it should take to push for social change.

Relatively small demonstrations began in Milwaukee in August of 1962 when twelve black high school students protested against A & P food stores' hiring practices. This was followed by small demonstrations against Marc's Big Boy restaurants in mid-1963, again over their failure to hire African Americans. In each case the firms backed down and agreed to hire blacks.[17] The escalation into major demonstrations began during the summer of 1963. Frank A. Aukofer, former Milwaukee journalist and author of *City With a Chance*, has identified four issues framing these early stages of Milwaukee's civil rights conflict: first, "[a] controversial appointment of a member of a commission set up to solve the city's racial and poverty problems;" second, "de facto segregation in the city's public schools;" third, "the membership of public officials in a segregated private club;" and finally, "open housing."[18]

The "controversial appointment" was to the Community Social Development Commission created by Mayor Henry Maier in 1962. This agency was intended to deal with inner city problems ranging from juvenile delinquency to the aged including, but somewhat avoiding, the sensitive issue of race. Shortly after its creation one of the

---

15   Patrick D. Jones, *The Selma of the North: Civil Rights Insurgency in Milwaukee* (Cambridge: Harvard University Press, 2009), 32.

16   Ibid., 36.

17   Julius Modlinski, "Commandos: A Study of a Black Organization's Transformation from Militant Protest to Social Service" (Ph. D. dissertation, University of Wisconsin-Madison, 1978), 59.

18   Frank A. Aukofer, *City With a Chance*" (Milwaukee: Bruce Publishing Company, 1968), 38.

members was quoted in local newspapers: "The Negroes look so much alike that you can't identify the ones that committed the crime" and "An awful mess of them have an IQ of zero."[19] Led by Milwaukee's newly created Congress of Racial Equality (CORE) chapter, protestors picketed the identified member's business, sat in at the county courthouse (the member in question was a county representative), phoned in to tie up the courthouse's telephone system, sat in the mayor's office, and in other ways demonstrated against the offending member and the Commission. CORE called off the demonstrations after around three weeks. Police arrested about two-dozen persons during these demonstrations. Little was accomplished, but CORE members and others gained experience in demonstrating, managing conflict, and civil disobedience.

The second issue of Milwaukee's civil rights conflicts, initiated in 1964, was more substantive: it surrounded the issue of de facto segregation in Milwaukee's schools. The NAACP, supported by CORE, and the newly formed Milwaukee United School Integration Committee (MUSIC) were the lead organizations. The issue driving this conflict was "intact busing"—that is busing black children to white schools and keeping them in separate classes (as well as taking them home for lunch so they would not eat in the school cafeteria).[20] This conflict took place on many fronts through sit-ins, school boycotts, legal action, school bus blockages, and other forms of civil disobedience. It was during these demonstrations that Father James Groppi first became active in local issues and developed a strong relationship with the NAACP Youth Council. Moreover, as Professor Jones argues, attorney Lloyd Barbee, a major figure behind the creation of MUSIC, began to expand the portfolio of direct action in Milwaukee through legal action as well as confrontations and demonstrations.[21]

It was during the conflicts over intact busing and school segregation that the NAACP Youth Council and Father James Groppi moved

19   Ibid., 39.

20   Jones, 65.

21   Jones, 78-79. For a more detailed history of the struggle for school integration, see James Kenneth Nelsen, "Racial Integration in the Milwaukee Public Schools, 1963-2003" (Ph.D. dissertation, University of Wisconsin-Milwaukee, 2003) and William Dahlk, Against the Wind: African Americans and the Schools of Milwaukee, 1963-2002 (Milwaukee: Marquette University Press, 2010).

into leadership roles in Milwaukee's civil rights movement. Nationally, the NAACP created youth councils in 1936, named initially as the Youth and College Division.[22] Perhaps the best known youth councils were in Oklahoma City where they conducted lunch counter demonstration, and in Milwaukee where they were among the key groups leading direct civil rights action. Many youth councils, including in Milwaukee, pursued educational and social goals starting during the 1950s and 1960s. Mrs. Ardie Halyard, an active NAACP member, organized Milwaukee's Youth Council in 1947. It was recognized as the NAACP's outstanding Youth Council in 1948.[23] The Youth Council consisted primarily of pre-teens and teens, and first became active in civil rights in late 1965.

Father James Groppi, a Milwaukee native, white Catholic priest, and community organizer, was based in St. Boniface Parish in the inner city, a parish originally serving Germans. In 1965, he marched in Selma, Alabama, and participated in the Southern Christian Leadership Conference voter registration project. Upon his return to Milwaukee he joined the protests as they gained momentum there, ultimately moving into a leadership role. Subsequently, he was named an advisor to the local Youth Council and was widely recognized as a militant civil rights leader, a rarity for a white in the country at this time.

It was also during the struggle over school integration that the relationship between police and segments of the black community, never good, worsened. As noted above, Harold Breier was appointed chief in 1964, just as civil rights direct action was gaining steam. Many black leaders pushed for the police to develop community relations programs; Breier countered by scoffing at the idea and developing a hard line response. Part of his response was to shift the attention of the MPD's vice squad of six to eight officers away from the traditional province of such units—prostitution, gambling, etc.—to civil rights organizations. Their operations consisted of overt surveillance: regularly following, photographing, and in other ways keeping tabs on civil rights activists and demonstrations—approaches seen by the activists as harassment and intimidation. Professor Jones quotes Father Groppi: "[Milwaukee police] followed us for something like six months. Everywhere we went! You got up in the morning, they were

22   "History of the NAACP Youth & College Division," accessed November 21, 2014, http://www.naacp.org.

23   Modlinski, 57-58.

there. You went to visit your family, they were there. You went out to a restaurant, they were there. You took someone to a movie, they were there."[24]

The third issue, raised in 1966 by the NAACP and its Youth Council, concerned the Fraternal Order of Eagles, a national organization that excluded blacks. It was in response to this issue that the NAACP Youth Council, with Father Groppi as its advisor, emerged as the leader of Milwaukee's civil rights protests. As Aukofer notes, the issue of Eagles membership was one of the least understood or popular civil rights issue.[25] Two values competed: first, the right to associate with whomever one wished in a private club coupled with the right of that club to select its own members; and second, the right of African Americans to participate in a club widely viewed as a semi-public organization, housing the political activities of major local, state, and national politicians as well as judges and other influential citizens.

The protests against the Eagles at first gained little media attention. Consequently protestors decided to change their strategy and target individuals at their residences. The first was a circuit court judge who lived in Wauwatosa, an older working class suburb of Milwaukee. This added a third value to the mix: the right of citizens to live in peace in their neighborhoods. These demonstrations attracted a large following, including counter protestors. Ultimately, as the threat and level of violence increased, Wauwatosa called for the National Guard to assist local police and county sheriffs. Adding to community tension, three Ku Klux Klan members bombed Milwaukee's NAACP headquarters during this period.

It was becoming clear that although the Youth Council and Groppi were advocates of non-violence, violence was increasingly threatening the safety of demonstrators. Also, many of the demonstrators were difficult to control. Out of these concerns, Father Groppi announced the creation of the Commandos in October of 1966. Aukofer describes their formation:

> Early in October, Father Groppi announced that the Youth Council had organized a commando unit, a direct action force of Negro youths who would handle "very tense situations." The new youth council commandos even had distinctive uniforms—army fatigues,

24   Jones, 149-150.

25   Aukofer, 97.

boots, and black berets.... Their main job was to function as policemen, to protect the youth council demonstrators and to keep order
on picket lines. But they also would conduct their own demonstrations where a situation was likely to get rough.[26]

As former Marquette University staffer Julius Modlinski points out
in his doctoral dissertation, the primary purposes of the Commandos
were to protect and discipline marchers, and to add the impression
of increased militancy on the part of the black community. The
Commandos believed that police protection was insufficient to protect the marchers; indeed, they believed that police often harassed
them. But also, the Commandos wanted to bring discipline to the
marchers, some of whom were just out "raising hell" rather than stick-
ing to principles of non-violence and peaceful demonstrations.[27] As
Professor Patrick Jones notes, their creation was met with conster-
nation: the *Milwaukee Journal* compared them to Hitler Youth and
the Red Guard; the *Sentinel* described them as a band of vigilantes;
and Milwaukee's adult NAACP quietly opposed the group's creation.
As Professor Jones explains: "Most white Milwaukeeans reacted to
the Commandos with a mix of surprise, fear, outrage, and opposition.
For many whites, the Commandos conjured up images of marauding
young black men undermining the rule of law and spreading racial
violence."[28] Like them or not, the Commandos were to become major
players in Milwaukee's civil rights conflicts.

Police viewed the creation of the Commandos as a provocation and
increased their surveillance and harassment (at least from the point of
view of activists). In the name of "protection" they observed Freedom
House, a residence that served as a meeting place for Youth Council
members and Commandos, day and night. When Groppi protested,
Breier responded: "In our [police] opinion, you need protection and
protection you're going to get, whether you like it or not." Four members of the youth council were arrested and fined for shooting dice
in a one-dollar game. A young woman was arrested for littering after
discarding a cigarette butt.[29] In response to police protection Youth

---

26   Ibid., 103.

27   Modlinski, 76-77; Jones, 131-142.

28   Ibid., 140-141.

29   Ibid., 151-152.

Council members and Commandos reciprocated by "protecting" Chief Breier's home. It was clear that tensions were increasing.

Nonetheless, after what seemed endless consultations, attempts at mediation, meetings, and the demonstrations, the issue of the Fraternal Order of Eagles faded. Several influential politicians and judges resigned their membership, but little else changed. The Youth Council and Father Groppi, however, announced that housing would be the next issue. It would later prove tumultuous and attract nation-wide attention. But before demonstrations over housing could begin, Milwaukee experienced a major riot.

THE 1967 RIOT AND DEMONSTRATIONS

From late July into early August 1967, riots broke out in Milwaukee, resulting in four deaths (three civilians and one police officer) and over 1,700 arrests. Their onset was not without warning. A bar fight spilled out into the street on a Saturday evening. When police responded the large crowd that gathered started breaking store windows. The community restlessness carried over to the next day when "a number of black adults who had been working with youth all summer reported ... that the events of early Sunday morning had sparked excited discussion and curiosity about what was 'going on' in the area."[30] Whether it would have helped or not, police rejected offers of help from youth workers. Later, as the disturbance increased, civil rights leaders attempted to intervene but again, their offers were refused.[31] Mayor Maier, however, responded swiftly, declaring a curfew and requesting that the National Guard be mobilized.

Although I lived in Milwaukee at the time, I was out of town during the entire disturbance and curfew period. It was only later as I got to know Robert Kliesmet and other leaders of the Milwaukee Police Association that I developed a perspective of the police action during the civil disturbance. From their point of view, the department was ill prepared to deal with such a disturbance. They had little training and were without proper equipment. Many police, believing themselves under fire, brought their own rifles to the job instead of relying on what they considered inadequate departmental weapons. (Hunting—especially deer hunting—is a very popular sport in Wisconsin.) Moreover,

30   Flaming, 45.

31   Flaming, 45-48.

according to union leaders, police spent a lot of time shooting at each other rather than active rioters.

Despite the loss of life and property, Milwaukee's riot was generally viewed as relatively mild compared to those in Detroit, Newark, and other major cities. Whether this was the result of a faster and/or more effective response by Mayor Maier and Chief Breier or the restraint and limited size of Milwaukee's African American community is not clear, and arguments can be made on both sides. Many in Milwaukee, however, believed that the police response during and immediately after the riots inflamed relations between police and the African-American community.

For example, a few days after the 1967 riot Chief Breier created the Tactical Enforcement Unit (the TAC unit), his primary response to the racial problems exploding in Milwaukee. The unit consisted of seven sergeants and forty-five patrol officers who were "to provide additional police service in the event of major incidents or disasters."[32] This unit was assigned ten cars, with three or four officers per car. Former TAC squad member Bob Connolly describes their staffing and functioning:

> Yes, August 7, 1967 was indeed a new day. Fifty-five of the biggest burliest guys the Milwaukee Police Department had to offer were placed together for one purpose. To regain and keep control of this city ... If you smarted off to the beat copy [sic], you didn't do it to these guys. Not unless you were looking for a bad time and wanted to find out just how fast you could wind up in jail. Just a discussion of these "tac guys" was enough to send the liberals scurrying for the hills. It didn't matter if you respected them or feared them, the Tactical Enforcement Unit demanded and quickly gained respect.[33]

---

32   Order No. 6074, Department of Police, City of Milwaukee, August 7, 1967. Former Milwaukee Police Captain Ken Henning, who has written an unpublished history of the MPD, claims that Milwaukee's TAC unit was the first SWAT (Special Weapons and Tactics) team in the United States. Former Los Angeles Police Department Chief Daryl Gates also claimed that distinction for his department. See Ken S. Henning, "History of the Milwaukee Police Department" (unpublished manuscript, undated), 23. See also Daryl F. Gates, *Chief: My Life in the LAPD* (New York: Bantam Books, July 1992). From the data available each emerged at about the same time, both in response to unrest in minority communities.

33   Bob Connolly, "Milwaukee Police Department Tactical Enforcement Unit" (unpublished memo, Association of SWAT Personnel, 1993).

The perception that the TAC unit was a tough squad, not to be messed with, polarized Milwaukeeans at that time. For many, TAC was a "goon squad" utilized to "keep blacks in their place;" for others TAC was a successful source of protection against illegal riotous behavior. Complicating the issue and playing into the "goon squad" depiction, TAC was an all-white, all-male unit. Not having female officers in 1967 was one thing: women were not allowed to do routine patrol work, let alone TAC or SWAT-like activities until the 1970s-1980s. But not having blacks in such units was another story. One explanation was that there were few blacks in the MPD at the time and the MPD leadership believed that they would be best utilized in black neighborhoods. This justification is troublesome. First, the TAC unit as mobilized in Milwaukee *was* working in black neighborhoods. Second, while having black police work black neighborhoods certainly has merit—black citizens would like to see themselves as among those policing as well as those being policed—it can be, and has been, used as a justification for keeping black police out of white neighborhoods, as well as ineligible for assignment to special units and for the promotions or "perks" that go with them.

The creation of a special response unit after the riot was probably necessary, especially given the poor performance as described by union leaders. Clearly the department needed a capacity to respond to threats of major disturbances properly equipped and trained. The problem was that Milwaukee's TAC squad operated as, and appeared like, an occupying force. Moreover, and equally troublesome, TAC was the only operational response to the riot and demonstrations. While community relations or other forms of outreach programs were generally believed in the police field to be of limited value, at least they represented to an alienated population that police departments were reaching out to them, attempting to somehow bridge the gap between police and blacks. Yet Breier was adamant that he knew best how to police Milwaukee; thus there would be no community relations programs. Behind this lay his deep suspicion: if the department would meet with community leaders, they would be meeting with communists and other ultra liberals.

In the midst of all this, the Youth Council and Groppi announced during late August of 1967 that they would initiate a campaign for an open housing ordinance in Milwaukee. This campaign produced the last and most violent set of demonstrations in the city. Although the state already had open housing legislation, it was generally considered toothless and unenforceable. To attract more attention than had earlier demonstrations, the plan was to move into different neighborhoods: specifically, marchers intended to go to the South Side of Milwaukee, basically an all-white working class area opposed to the civil rights movement.

The significance of the demonstrators' decision to march to the South Side of Milwaukee lay in geography. The city is divided into north and south sides by a huge river valley spanned only by a couple of viaducts. Entrance to the south side then required using one of these viaducts. North-siders and South-siders rarely crossed them. It seemed almost as if Milwaukee was divided into two distinct cities.[34] The first march took place on Monday August 28, 1967; the second, the next night. In his doctoral dissertation, Julius Modlinski describes the events, beginning when

> [a] contingent of Youth Council protestors and Commandos marched to Milwaukee's south side. Hecklers and counter demonstrators immediately began to react. There were several arrests, and 22 reported injuries. The following night, Tuesday, August 29th, the situation seriously worsened and crowds in excess of 10,000 gathered along the route to and in the area of Kosciuszko Park, located in the heart of the city's south side. The approximately 250 marchers were bombarded with debris (bottles, eggs, beer cans, stones, cherry bombs, pieces of wood, etc.). By the time the march ended, some two and one-half hours later, 45 marchers and counter demonstrators had been arrested and another 22 injured. Sometime during that evening, Freedom House, used by the Youth Council members and Commandoes as a place for small informal gatherings, had been severely damaged by fire. Youth Council members and neighborhood residents blamed the police for this, claiming that the fire had started when a tear gas canister was fired into the small wooden structure. Police denied the story.[35]

Then-*Milwaukee Journal* reporter Frank Aukofer describes the events and the police response as the marchers approached their destination, Kosciuszko Park:

---

34   As a teen, I probably crossed to the Milwaukee's South Side less than a dozen times and, in each case, it was to go roller-skating at Milwaukee's only rink.

35   Modlinski, 89.

[A]lmost as if on a signal—a mob of whites surged into the intersection a block away to the east and rushed toward the open housing marchers. At least a thousand persons were in the white mass,
and by the time police realized what was happening, it already was
too late to stop them. The mob swarmed around the police and the
marchers, who were huddled against building on the north side-
walk behind commandos. The commandos had stepped forward to
face the attack.

Some of the whites rocked a squad car while others tossed eggs
and other debris at Father Groppi and the other demonstrators.
There was pandemonium—a riot by any definition.

The police recovered quickly. A group armed with shotguns
pointed their weapons at the sky and fired them as fast as they
could pump fresh shells into the chambers. The fusillade startled
the crowd as, almost simultaneously, other policemen tossed or shot
tear gas bombs into the mob.[36]

But the conflict was not yet over, for demonstrators had to get back to
and across the viaduct. And police, the Commandos, and demonstrators literally had to fight their way to the viaduct. Aukofer notes after
the demonstrators had made it to the safety of the viaduct:

> In one of his rare tributes to police, Father Groppi commented that
> he thought they had done as good a job protecting the marchers as
> was possible under the circumstance. ..."In all the demonstrations
> I covered, I never observed police hostility to the marchers or any
> evidence that they wanted to harm them. They worked to keep the
> peace and fend off any hostility. ... At least Breier allowed his offi-
> cers to act professionally."[37]

Nonetheless, Groppi and the Youth Council got their wish for more
attention: "Platoons of reporters from newspapers and broadcasters
around the country parachuted into Milwaukee to cover the story."[38]

Things continued to heat up in the fall of 1967 as ongoing demonstrations gathered nationwide attention. Groups from Chicago and
NAACP representatives from Kentucky, Indiana, Illinois, Ohio,
Michigan, and West Virginia joined marches in a large September
demonstration.[39] Hostile mobs confronted demonstrators. At the

36   Aukofer, 115.
37   Ibid., 116.
38   Ibid., 111.
39   Modlinski, 251.

same time the Black Panthers began to challenge the Commandos for dominance in Milwaukee's civil rights movement, while internal schisms developed in the Youth Council with some Council members objecting to Groppi's role. The American Nazi party held a South-Side rally. Vice President Hubert Humphrey met with Groppi and several Commandos. Wisconsin's governor and other major political figures called on Milwaukee's Common Council to pass an open housing ordinance—to no avail.

The Youth Council and the Commandos increasingly complained about police harassment. Then in early October, police and Commandos had a major confrontation in which police blocked the path of demonstrators, demonstrators who resisted were arrested, a shotgun blast took out a window of a police car while an officer was in the car, and thirty-nine marchers and two police were hospitalized. Adding to all this, civil rights leaders and the Commandos believed that Milwaukee's police were becoming increasingly disrespectful, confrontational, and violent. In response the Commandoes planned a confrontation they knew would result in aggressive police action, which they planned to meet with major resistance. The confrontation was planned to take place in a major intersection. The Commandos blocked the intersection, anticipating a police charge with riot sticks in hand. When the police charged, the Commandos responded violently, striking back as best they could. In the ruckus twenty-one Commandos and six police officers were hospitalized. According to the leadership of the Commandos, this resulted in more respect and judicious use of force from the police in the future.[40] The Commandos were bruised and battered, but for them standing up to police was a source of great pride.[41]

---

40 Ibid., 249-259.

41 After I began working with the Commandos, I heard about this confrontation many times. Although committed to non-violence in the overall civil rights movement, Commando leaders believed that their violent response to what they perceived of as police harassment led to a more stable relationship between them and police.

AN END TO DEMONSTRATIONS AND A
TRANSFORMATION: WORK WITH THE
COMMANDOS

Both the Youth Council and demonstrators were growing tired from protests, especially the Commandos who had borne the brunt of the most recent conflict and violence. (One can believe that police felt the same way.) They believed that they had made a powerful statement to the community, had maintained integrationist and non-violent values, and earned the respect (if not the liking) of police. Many believed that the marches and demonstrations had made their point, and new approaches were called for. Moreover, many Commandos believed that Martin Luther King, Father Groppi, and the civil rights movement had profoundly changed their personal lives and could change the lives of others as well. They wanted to get on with their lives: many were unemployed, some married. Some were resentful that certain African Americans who had stood on the sidelines during the demonstrations were now grabbing good jobs created by the money flowing into Milwaukee as a result of the demonstrations and riots, while criticizing the Commandos for wanting to back away from demonstrations. But also the Commandos wanted to stick together, maintaining the ties that had developed among them.[42]

Under the guidance of Jules Modlinski, a staff member at Marquette University, and Wesley Scott, the Executive Director of Milwaukee's Urban League, the Commandos decided that they could use their experiences to influence youth positively, especially those prone to trouble. As in most major cities, funds were becoming available for special projects undertaken by "indigeous" citizens. Both Scott and Modlinski were keenly aware of the potential of the Commandos to provide leadership and the availability of funds. In the spring of 1968 Modlinski called me and asked if I would meet with a group of Commandos who were older, most of whom were out of work and yet who wanted to develop a program for troubled youth. Modlinski later indicated that he contacted me because we had worked well together at a conference, I had a working relationship with Wisconsin's Division of Corrections, and because I had some reputation as a grant writer. I was eager and a time was set for me to meet with the "Big Nine" of the Commandos.

---

42   These were my own personal impressions once I had started to work
     with the Commandos.

We met at the Urban League. The Big Nine were already there and seated. Wes Scott, the Urban League's director, introduced me and left. Hank Walters, the Commando leader at the time, opened the conversation, describing their desire to move on to activities beyond demonstrating, the impact that civil rights had on them, and their belief that they had something to offer younger people coming up, especially troubled youths with the same backgrounds they had. Walters also said that funds were available for such programs and they were looking for someone who could write proposals. Modlinski and Scott had suggested me. Was I interested? Could I write a proposal? If I could, how long would it take?

My answer to Walters was yes, I was interested, very interested—and yes, I could write a proposal. It would take a week or two for me to do so. It took several meetings over a couple of weeks, however, to come to agreement. My stance was that I was eager to help them but we had to be clear what each side got out of it: they would get jobs and I wanted eventually to write about them. Their initial stance was that they wanted to work with me, but as a secret organization they did not want any public exposure. We ultimately compromised: I wouldn't write about them for a long time (left undefined) and I would write grants for them.

They got the grant, the first of many. In the following years the Commandos, organized as Commando Project I, thrived. To develop and maintain organizational credibility and to avoid any possibility of abuse of funds, the Urban League, at first and later Milwaukee's Chamber of Commerce, handled these funds. By 1978, the Commandos ran an array of programs that involved counseling youths, finding employment, creating an alternative high school, running a group foster home, employing youth during the summer, and sponsoring camp, recreation, and family programs.

POLICING AND RACE IN MILWAUKEE

Not unlike in other American cities, and as is apparent in the above account, trouble began brewing between the MPD and the black community in Milwaukee well before Breier's reign. In 1960, for example, a report to Mayor Frank Zeidler documented some of the complaints and tensions at that time. The report found "significant areas of misunderstandings and tension" between the police and residents of the inner core. The tensions and misunderstandings include complaints that some police officers were not aware of "cultural factors related to such things as loitering and fun-seeking behavior."[43]

Yet, throughout his career and during this era of great social change, Chief Breier was unyielding. He knew best; no one could challenge him; his opponents were leftist liberals, communists, and criminals. None of this meant that many police and mid-level managers, and even the police union, did not try to quietly establish some kind of behind the scenes working relationship with elements of the black community. In one example, I arranged for the leadership of both the Commandos and police union to meet outside of Milwaukee to discuss their problems of working together. This was at a time that the Black Panthers were attempting to challenge the Commandos' leadership in Milwaukee. The Panthers insisted on a fairly radical version of black power; the Commandos were firmly committed to Martin Luther King's vision of a unified, integrated America. The Commandos were able to brief police on what the issues were and how conflict might ensue.[44] Another example was how to handle warrant service if any of the Commandos (not just the big nine but the entire group) was to be served by the MPD. The agreement was that the police would serve the warrant at the Commando office and the Commandos would assure that it would be served and followed up on. Both were attempts to create back channels of communication to reduce conflict: I suspect that there were others. I have no idea whether Breier had any inkling of these arrangements. If he did, he ignored them.

Yet as Breier wound down his career he became, if anything, more irascible: busing was exporting crime to Milwaukee's south side; community relations and community policing were retreats from good policing. Breier was an ardent defender of the status quo. As John Gurda said to me: "He spoke for a Milwaukee that worked in the past, but was gone; a police department that worked well in that world but not

---

43 "Final Report to the Honorable Frank P. Zeidler, Mayor" (unpublished report, Mayor's Study Committee on Social Problems in the Inner Core Area of the City, April 1960), quoted in Flaming, 31.

44 The attempts by the Black Panthers to establish a foothold in Milwaukee were largely quashed by the Commandos. I believe this was due to the fact that the population that likely might have been Panthers had already been recruited as Commandos, inspired by Groppi and Martin Luther King. As noted several times, the Commandos were very tough guys.

in the changing world of the 1960s on. He spoke for a high moral purpose of another age, and was a moral man in those terms."[45]

Little changed for years after Breier retired. A 1991 study of community attitudes towards police, conducted by DMT & S and summarized in a report for Mayor John Norquist's Citizen Commission on Police-Community Relations, found that "the majority of Milwaukee residents believed that the MPD did a good job of controlling crime, and that residents of all races and age groups were willing to call on police for help." Yet like the 1960 report to Mayor Zeidler discussed above:

> [T]he consultants found great racial polarization between Whites and African-Americans…on ratings of the relationship between the MPD and the African-American community; on belief that officers use more force when restraining and arresting minority suspects; on belief that the MPD treats minorities worse than whites; and on belief that officers are honest, cooperative, or have the public's best interest at heart.[46]

As best can be determined, these beliefs persisted well into the twenty-first century—the tragedy being that most in the African American community want and need good policing and that most police want to provide it. It was out of such beliefs that community policing emerged. But before we delve into community policing, the chapter that follows explores two other elements of the Breier legacy that would have an enormous impact on the ability to shift police strategies: an aggressive and empowered police union and persistence of the detective culture, with its opposition to crime prevention.

---

45   John Gurda, interview by George Kelling, February 21, 2012.

46   "A Report to Mayor John Q. Norquist and the Board of Fire and Police Commissioners" (unpublished report of The Mayor's Citizen Commission on Police-Community Relations, October 15, 1991), 10.

CHAPTER FOUR

BREIER'S LEGACY IN THE MILWAUKEE POLICE DEPARTMENT AND MILWAUKEE

Although Harold Breier retired in 1984, in many respects he "owned" the Milwaukee Police Department for decades later. Breier deserves ample credit for leaving the MPD a highly disciplined organization in terms of the internal mores and manners of policing: dress, deference to authority, internal discipline, and absence of financial and political corruption. Yet his legacy included a troubled relationship between police and minorities in the community, especially African Americans, as we have seen. Furthermore Breier's orientation around detectives meant that he tended to demean the valuable work of patrol officers. What was equally ominous for the future of the MPD was the growth under his administration of an empowered adversarial police union, one that would be more inclined to work against police leadership in the future. This would be especially significant when external police leadership was sought by city officials in the years following Breier's administration.

Breier's intransigence in many areas led the MPD to ignore and even resist many of the positive changes taking place nationally in policing—toward a community policing model, for instance. This was the future of American policing; yet Breier's actions held the MPD back from joining the new professional movement. It would be decades before the Milwaukee police could hope to reclaim a position at the forefront of American policing.

REVISITING THE DETECTIVE CULTURE
IN THE MPD

Part of the problem with Breier's shaping of the MPD lay in the fact that he was a detective through and through. Over a police career that spanned forty-four years, Breier spent only three as other than a detective—during his first years on the force while he was still cutting his teeth on policing. As soon as he was eligible he became an acting detective; he never again left the detective bureau. As chief Breier never wore a uniform. His daughter, Suzanne Breier, suggested that Breier preferred not to wear the chief's uniform "because he felt it pretentious."[1] Yet Breier never denied the trappings of office: his desk was on an elevated platform, towering over staff or guests. The willing and voluble Inspector Breier was always a favorite of reporters looking for a good interview. Nobody would have accused Chief Breier of being shy about himself, his office, or its privileges. His refusal to wear a uniform says something far more profound about his chosen identity. He was first and foremost a detective.

Breier's detective background explains a great deal about his views of policing. Detectives dressed in civilian clothes; controlled most of their own time and agenda; operated with considerable mystique; were considered (and often were) the best and the brightest; and were often glamorized in media and fiction.[2] They were organizational elites

1   Ronald H. Snyder, "Chief for Life: Harold Breier and His Era" (Ph.D. dissertation, University of Wisconsin-Milwaukee, December 2002), 186n11.

2   The idea of detectives as the elites of policing had its origins in at least two sources: detective fiction and the public relations activities of the Federal Bureau of Investigation under J. Edgar Hoover. These stories are fascinating in their own right but not central to our story here. Briefly, the notion of the investigator as having a special capacity for ratiocination has its origins in Charles Dickens' Inspector Bucket in *Bleak House*, Edgar Allen Poe's C. Auguste Dupin in *The Murders in the Rue Morgue*, and Sir Conan Doyle's Sherlock Holmes. In this view, detectives had special skills both in observation and in exact reasoning and deduction. The detective as the pinnacle of public policing, however, was the product of J. Edgar Hoover who took over a troubled, corrupt Bureau of Investigation during the 1920s and turned it into the prestigious Federal Bureau of Investigation (FBI). In a sense local police took on the FBI's mantle during the early 1930s and 1940s, shifting their emphasis from crime prevention to law enforcement (that is, responding to crime after it occurs). In this model, detectives are genuine professionals. Consequently, even to this day, although police recruits can't

whose core mission was solving crimes through complicated ratiocination. Patrol officers on the other hand were "grunts" who took reports and conducted routine activities. This entrenched ideology was nearly impossible for subsequent chiefs to confront: from the Breier era forward the MPD was effectively divided into two distinct departments, detectives and patrol, and to the extent that they overlapped it was under the control of detectives.[3]

The best example of this occurred during the last years of the Hegerty administration when plans were made to create new district and squad areas. The chief of the CIB (Criminal Investigation Bureau) headed the effort and detectives dominated the working group, both in numbers and influence, much to the resentment of patrol leadership. A draft report about detectives highlights the view of the CIB patrol commanders: "The CIB was operating as a closed organizational system, failing to coordinate resources with district commanders and failing to adequately share information relative to criminal investigations that directly impacted neighborhoods for which district commanders were responsible for policing"[4] Other concerns regarding the CIB included what was seen as excessive overtime—driven by extensive daily briefings and court time; the evolution of a "caste" system within the CIB in which friendships and "who you knew" controlled assignments; and the extent to which the CIB refused to capitalize on new information technology both for crime analysis and information storage relying instead on pen and paper systems.

The detective culture that pervaded MPD rested upon a misunderstanding and misrepresentation of the work both of patrol officers and detectives. In reality patrol officers regularly dealt with complex problems; detectives often busied themselves with routine paper work. Comprehending this reality was crucial to moving forward with the community policing model that began to evolve in the United States beginning in the 1980s. It would demand full recognition of the roles

---

wait to get into their uniforms once they join police departments; after a couple of years they can't wait to get out of them and become detectives (or, if they can't make detective, into a plain clothes unit).

3   Group interviews with MPD command staff (that included former and current CIB leadership) and observations of their meetings by George Kelling, 2011-2013.

4   James Harpole, "Reform of the Milwaukee Police Department's Criminal Investigation Bureau," draft report, no date.

and responsibilities of patrol officers on the streets in preventing crime, forming strong relationships with citizens in local communities, and gaining knowledge of street level activities. It would demand that detectives begin to think about individual crimes in terms of larger sets of problems, and work with patrol officers and local community members to address the problems as well as solve crimes.

THE PPA: FROM PROFESSIONAL ASSOCIATION TO ADVERSARIAL POLICE UNION

It was during the administration of Harold Breier that the Milwaukee police union became a powerful force, both inside the MPD and politically. My introduction to police unions, indeed my first hands-on experience with policing itself, came about in the late 1960s when I met Robert Kliesmet, an older student in the evening class "Introduction to Criminal Justice" that I was teaching at UW-Milwaukee. After a class one night Bob approached me, identified himself as the president of Milwaukee's Professional Police Association (PPA), and asked if I would join him to have a beer and talk about some of the problems of the MPD. I said yes—and so began my own relationship with the Milwaukee Police Department and the Milwaukee Police Union. Over the next two decades, I would have the opportunity to work with, observe, and to some degree influence the development of the PPA. Because of this relationship, the account I present here is admittedly personal and reflective as well as analytical.

Early Years of the PPA: Recognizing the Nature of Police Work

When we sat down to talk, Kliesmet's starting line—aggressive in his usual fashion—was: "Are you only going to write grants for the Commandos?" By this time my work with the group was well known in Milwaukee. Uncertain as to what Bob was after, I indicated that I was prepared to write proposals for others as well. Bob then opened up: "We're getting killed out there. Breier and his command staff sit at their downtown desks pontificating that they won't meet with citizen groups and every day those of us on the streets are running into more and more anger. Bosses don't have to face them, we do. Police have to start talking to black groups and explain what we're doing. We'd like you to write a grant for the union to start a community relations program."

At first I hesitated: I was enjoying work with the Commandos and did not want to jeopardize that relationship. At the same time, working with Milwaukee's Professional Police Association could be an opportunity as well. The problem was that the PPA and Commandos, at least on the surface, appeared to be enemies. I explained that I would like to work with the PPA but would have to talk to the Commando leadership about it. When I did, the Commando leaders were initially surprised but ultimately did not object to my working with the PPA. I made clear to both organizations that any discussion about the other was off limits; the arrangement worked and I was able to maintain strong relations with each group. I believed from the outset that each had a vested self-interest in maintaining a peaceful, if not admiring, relationship with the other.

Subsequently I wrote a community relations grant proposal for the union that was submitted to both state and federal agencies. It was never funded and I never learned why: perhaps the proposal was not well written; perhaps it was seen as undermining the MPD; there may have been anti-union bias on the part of funders; perhaps union involvement in community relations was not perceived of as appropriate (and maybe it was not). Nevertheless, writing the proposal did give me a unique opportunity to see things from the point of view of police unions and line patrol officers. Milwaukee union leaders seemed sincere in their belief that police officers were endangered by Breier's maintenance of a remote if not hostile relationship with the African American community, and by his reluctance to meet with groups interested in improving police community relations. I came to believe that police officers had a point of view that should be heard by the community.

As my relationship with the PPA matured the union regularly asked me to testify on their behalf in binding arbitration, which I did four or five times, both during Kliesmet's tenure as president or secretary/treasurer and then under his successor, Brad Debraska. I insisted upon a narrow scope in my testimony—focusing on salary—that grew out of my view that the complexity of police work and the ubiquity and importance of officer use of discretion justified higher salaries. What struck me most the first time I testified, probably during the late 1960s or early 1970s, was that Milwaukee's job classification system was badly organized: it ranked the complexity of police work on a par with that of assistant bookbinders and paid police accordingly, which to me reflected a gross misunderstanding of the nature of police work by city officials.

I still recall the dismay of union board members when they first learned of my intention to focus on complexity and discretion as the justification for reclassifying police work and adjusting salary levels. When testifying, I usually came into Milwaukee the night before to have dinner with Kliesmet, the PPA board, and their attorney. Generally we would have dinner at the Schroeder Hotel (now the downtown Hilton). After dinner and rounds of police "war stories," the conversation would turn to my plans for testifying. I made clear that I would not testify about issues over which I strongly disagreed with police unions, such as early retirement or many work-related matters. I also indicated that my focus would be on current salary levels and the need to line police salaries up with occupations of similar complexity and responsibility. As I talked about these issues, board members would roll their eyes: for them such subjects were abstract and academic. Instead, they wanted me to justify increased salaries on the basis of police heroism and risk-taking. They had bought hook, line, and sinker what their training and Breier had told them: that policing was simple and routine law enforcement. If someone broke the law, they were arrested; if someone didn't break the law, they had nothing to fear from police. In fact this characterization simply did (and does) not represent the real world of policing. Police deal with myriad problems ranging from neighborhood disputes, to lost children, to the proverbial "cats in trees," to bank robberies, to domestic violence. In handling such problems police choose from a range of options for taking action: offering warnings, help, education, counseling, and referrals; only occasionally do they make arrests. Yet the significance and degree of discretion exercised by police in handling such problems went unrecognized in the world of unionists at this time. The evenings generally ended with disheartened board members shaking their heads, slumped in their chairs, convinced that Kliesmet had seriously erred in getting me to be a key witness.

The next day as I began testifying their attitudes had not changed: here was an out-of-touch academic talking about abstract issues to justify their most critical issue—higher salaries. But as my testimony began to roll out, one by one board members sat up straight, pulled in closer to the table, leaned forward, and increasingly nodded in agreement. As I used concrete examples, some from their war stories of the night before, many heard a view of their job they never had before: law enforcement was a small part of their job; they routinely dealt with complicated issues like domestic violence; they had to make complex decisions about how to enter a dispute, manage it, terminate it, and end the interaction. After my testimony they responded with enthusiastic comments and questions: why didn't they know about this? Why wasn't "use of discretion" taught in the police academy?

In fact, Milwaukee police and Breier himself were not at all unusual in their ignorance about police use of discretion. Until well into the 1960s the dominant view in American policing failed to recognize the existence and pervasiveness of police discretion in handling problems and the need for managing it. The problem in Milwaukee was that this view persisted until well into the 1980s. The fact that the PPA continued to ask me to testify on their behalf meant that they understood and put considerable value in the ideas of complexity and discretion. A significant indicator of this development in their thinking emerged when one year I persuaded them to include police officer stratification as one of the demands. By this is meant that line police officers would be able to attain promotion within a rank from, for example, assistant police officer or police officer one (the first year or two for rookies), to associate police officer or police officer two (three to five years), to a senior police officer who would operate with considerable autonomy, train young officers, and "own" a geographical area. As such, a senior officer could be on a salary par with a sergeant. The Los Angeles Police Department has had a variation of this model for some time. Unfortunately, this demand was never met. Nonetheless, from my point of view it represented a new sophistication on the part of union leaders about the role of line police and the steps potentially important to the true professionalization of police.

THE DEVELOPMENT OF
AMERICAN POLICE UNIONS

Regardless of one's perspective on police unions, they were and are interesting entities. Their origins lay in police fraternal, benevolent, and social clubs that formed after the Civil War as a result of the ethnic and political affinities of police officers, and out of a need to provide relief to sick or disabled police. Police entrance into the labor movement was tumultuous during the late nineteenth and early twentieth centuries. At first, organized labor was not enthusiastic about police joining their ranks, a remnant of hostile police-union confrontations from earlier decades. As early as 1887, the American Federation of Labor (AFL) rejected the formation of a police council. In 1919, that decision was reversed and thirty-seven police unions were admitted to the AFL. Nevertheless Samuel Gompers, then president of the AFL, admonished that police should not be allowed to strike.

Early twentieth-century police reformers like August Vollmer as well as chiefs and commissioners vociferously opposed attempts at police unionization and sought to eliminate them. The idea of unions cut to the heart of reformers' struggles to wrest control of police departments from politicians and bring rank-and-file officers under a chief's administrative purview. In the view of reformers the military model, a tenet of early twentieth-century police reform, made unions inconceivable: police could no more be unionized than soldiers. Reformers made their objections to unionism stick. Chiefs threatened to fire police union organizers or members, as did Commissioner E. U. Curtis of Boston in 1919, triggering the infamous Boston police strike that saw days of riots and mayhem.[5] It is safe to say that the Boston strike shaped the debate about police unions in the United States, demolished the incipient police union movement, and shattered the relationship between organized labor and police associations. Following this strike, the AFL revoked all police charters. What remained of the early twentieth- century union movement was local fraternal organizations, often led by chiefs or other managers. Even the Fraternal Order of Police (FOP) was unable to recruit locals into a national fraternal organization, confronted as local members were with threats of firing if they dared affiliate with any national group.

The forces arrayed against police unionism held sway until well after World War II. Sporadic attempts to unionize police continued to be quashed by threats of and actual firings. During the 1940s, when officers again attempted to associate their locals with national unions (e.g., the American Federation of State County and Municipal Employees—AFSCME), the anti-union militancy of chiefs persisted and largely reigned. The *Police Chiefs' News Letter* (the predecessor to *Police Chief*, the publication of the International Association of Chiefs of Police, the IACP) noted in 1947 that ten police departments were

5   Robert Fogelson, *Big City Police* (Cambridge: Harvard University Press, 1977) 194.

unionized, with only four having dues check-offs (pay-roll deduction of union dues): Omaha, Tacoma, Duluth, and Flint.[6] At the same time those who joined unions were given thirty days in Los Angeles and two weeks in St. Louis to sever all relations with unions. Those few officers who refused were fired. Similar scenarios played out in Detroit, Chicago, and other cities.[7]

Few today recall just how far administrative control extended over police officers in those days. Officers had to live within a certain distance of police stations; they were restricted from living in the areas they policed; they had to carry weapons while off-duty; had their financial and sexual lives monitored and regulated; had no appeal process if and when disciplined; and in some cities, officers had to take police cars home with them.[8] During the 1960s, however, the national political climate regarding public unions changed. As firefighters, teachers, and other groups successfully organized, some local police organizations began to break through the barriers to unionization. Still police organizations, even when recognized as unions during the 1970s, remained relatively weak and underfunded.

FROM PROFESSIONAL ASSOCIATION TO POLICE UNION IN MILWAUKEE

In Milwaukee, as in many other cities, the driving force behind officers' desire to unionize was authoritarian and arbitrary police personnel practices. Wisconsin authorized cities to negotiate with police associations in 1960; yet the move had little impact on Milwaukee or the MPD. At the time Milwaukee's police union was weak. Kliesmet, who would become leader of the union in 1969, describes the PPA during the 1960s as little more than a fraternal organization dominated by "bosses—who weren't about to take on the chief." Furthermore Breier dismissed virtually every union request: for example, elimination of the requirement to wear neckties during the summer; recognition of higher education for officers; establishment of a counseling program for troubled officers; agreement to negotiations regarding rules; and acceptance of the right of officers to engage in off-duty political

6   *Police Chiefs' News Letter* 13, n. 8 (August 1947): 3.

7   Fogleson, 195.

8   Malcolm K. Sparrow, Mark H. Moore, and David M. Kennedy, *Beyond 911: A New Era for Policing* (New York: Basic Books, 1990), 36-37.

activity. In effect Breier created a "Catch 22": the chief makes the rules; one of the rules is that officers cannot discuss rules with outsiders, even city officials; ergo, the rules can't be part of collective bargaining.[9] Kliesmet remains adamant in his view that Breier's authoritarian rule drove union development. He contends that Breier could have significantly lessened union influence, both during its formative years and after, through a willingness to soften his authoritative administration.[10] Athough Breier's authoritarian style was not all that unique in the pre-1960s era, it was outdated by the 1960s. But Breier refused to change his stance.

Facing ongoing opposition from Breier and ineffective action by the PPA, in 1968 Kliesmet (while still a patrol officer) and three colleagues decided to challenge the leadership of the PPA by presenting a petition signed by 800 officers demanding a union voice regarding rules and regulations. The board of the PPA turned the petition down. Kliesmet and the other three petitioners were arrested immediately after the meeting and transported in a police wagon to headquarters where they were to be booked for "drunk and disorderly conduct"—a fabricated charge. A lieutenant intervened and stopped the booking, but warned the four that they shouldn't talk about what happened. Kliesmet, however, became (in)famous: elected to the PPA board late in 1968, he led a purge of the "bosses" from the board.

The conflict between the newly militant union and Breier intensified. Infuriated by Breier's refusal to negotiate in any real sense, the rank and file of the MPD called for a blue flu epidemic starting January 7, 1971. Breier, of course, heard of this in advance and attempted to preempt the strike. At the January 6 late shift role call (11 p.m.), he ordered any officers who called in sick after midnight to have to have doctors' excuses. In response the entire late shift walked out, starting the strike before midnight to defeat Breier's order. Kliesmet to this day believes that this act by Breier actually strengthened what was at the beginning merely a jittery determination on the part of the rank and file to walk out.[11] The strike lasted four days. The city remained calm during the entire episode and the PPA gained little; in fact, during the

9   Snyder, 40.

10   Robert Kliesmet, interview by George Kelling, February 1, 2012.

11   Ibid.

strike Kleismet said to me at one point, more than half seriously, "We better get back to work before citizens realize they don't miss us."

Moving to challenge Breier head on, the PPA board then decided to exercise what they considered to be their right to endorse political candidates. Breier responded by disciplining the eight board members still on police duty status. Kliesmet, the ninth board member, was on leave as the MPD-PPA liaison and therefore outside Breier's administrative reach. The union attempted to gain support through the Wisconsin Employment Relations Commission (WERC)—a state agency authorized to mediate conflicts between labor and management—and with court action. Although both WERC and the courts were supportive of the union's position and urged the chief to establish procedures to negotiate rules and regulations, Breier continued to stonewall. Local politicians, also sympathetic to the union's demands, were not prepared to deal with the political ramifications of contradicting Breier. In response to a court order Breier finally did offer a procedure for bargaining. Historian Ronald Snyder describes it:

> Under the proposal he [Breier] would be required to notify the police union of any proposed rule changes. If the union objected, negotiations would be held. If agreement was not reached within thirty days, the rule would automatically take effect. If, however, the union initiated a proposed rule change, the chief or his designated representative would enter into negotiations. If agreement was not reached within thirty days, the union's proposed rules change would be dropped.[12]

In other words, except for the drama of negotiations, nothing would change. The union remained powerless. Undaunted, Kliesmet and his PPA board colleagues turned to the Wisconsin State Legislature and successfully lobbied for a law ordering Milwaukee to adopt binding arbitration as the final step in resolving conflict. In Kliesmet's view, this was the most successful achievement of his career. In 1973 an arbitrator concluded that a grievance procedure should be adopted and rules and regulations negotiated. Finally, Breier's absolute power was curtailed.

Kliesmet and the union leadership, however, remained ambivalent about Breier. The "deal" that Breier had made to protect officers from outside inspection was a powerful force in the MPD and the PPA.

---

12   Snyder, 47.

As hard as the union fought regarding rules and regulations, they staunchly opposed any efforts to limit Breier's term in office. Kliesmet still recalls, with respect, a call from Breier thanking him and the union board for opposing proposals to limit his term in office. Meantime, police unions across the country moved to gain more power—locally, at the state level, and nationally. In 1973, the AFL-CIO went full circle, granting a charter to a breakaway group from the International Conference of Police Associations led by "Eddie" Kiernan (former president of the New York Police Benevolent Association). Kliesmet succeeded Kiernan as president of the breakaway group, the AFL-CIO International Union of Police Associations, leaving the local scene in 1983.

A number of lessons can be gleaned from Milwaukee's experience with the police union. The most important point here is that Breier's recalcitrance gave birth to a powerful and skillful union with experience in conflict as well as in developing alternative routes to success—through the WERC, the courts, the Common Council, the Fire and Police Commission, and the state legislature. But the Milwaukee police union account also illustrates the dissimilarities between public and private sector unions. As former Yale Law School Professor Clyde Summers, a strong advocate of public sector unions, explained: "[I]n private employment collective bargaining is a process of private decision making shaped primarily by market forces, while in public employment it is a process of governmental decision making shaped ultimately by political forces."[13] This distinction is fundamental to understanding how police unions operate. More specifically it is crucial to comprehending how the PPA gained power and influence. Ultimately the Milwaukee police union defeated Breier through political activity. As part of police unionization during the 1970s at least three procedures were adopted and utilized by unions seeking to affect political processes: direct two-party negotiations, grievance proceedings, and dues check-offs. In Milwaukee it was the second of these—grievance proceedings (binding arbitration to resolve disputes)—that was key to ultimately overthrowing Harold Breier's authoritarian rule. And if

13 Clyde W. Summers, "Public Employee Bargaining: A Political Perspective," *Yale Law Journal* 83 (1974): 1156. See also Lee C. Shaw and R. Theodore Clark. Jr., "The Practical Differences Between Public and Private Sector Collective Bargaining," *University of California Los Angeles Law Review* 19 (1972): 867.

collective bargaining in the public sector is a process shaped by politics, it is important to recognize that Breier gave the PPA a lot of practice in developing political skills. As we shall see in the next chapter, the PPA used this skill as a formidable opponent to change under later chiefs, especially during the Arreola administration.

In the meantime, Breier was also isolating Milwaukee police professionally, ignoring, if not debunking, the development and innovations occurring around the country. Even before Breier was appointed chief the verities of policing had begun to erode. The strategy of policing developed during the 1920s and 1930s with Milwaukee in its lead had reduced police corruption and political influence in the operation of police departments, and had established a coherent set of police tactics. By Breier's term in office the weakness and ultimately failure of this strategy were becoming clearer; nevertheless, he steadfastly resisted change. In doing so, Breier prevented both the MPD and the city back from participating in and reaping the benefits of a new model—community policing.

PROFESSIONAL ISOLATION FROM THE
BEST OF CONTEMPORARY POLICING

The 1970s and 1980s were momentous years for American policing. In a sense these two decades were polar opposites. The period of the 1970s was extraordinarily discouraging for police. Despite their high hopes for car-based police tactics—preventive patrol and rapid response to calls for service—by the late 1970s police had to confront the reality that their core competencies simply did not work. Crime was soaring, the African American community continued to resent how policing was conducted, and no promising tactics seemed in the offing. Many chiefs simply threw up their hands: crime was out of their control; they could respond after crimes were committed but until society changed there was little else they could do. The 1980s, however, were a decade of promise: problem solving, broken windows, and collaboration entered the police vocabulary—all integrated during the decade into what became known as community policing. Chiefs like Lee Brown in Houston, William Bratton in Boston, Willie Williams in Philadelphia, Ed Davis in Lowell, Massachusetts, Ed Flynn in Chelsea, Massachusetts, and others began experimenting with community policing. They confronted myriad issues: handling calls for service; making needed changes in departmental structures and administration; managing the responses of police unions; developing new metrics for measuring success in community policing; and so on.

Two questions beg answering: how did we get to a policing strategy that largely failed? What happened that a host of new ideas emerged (and some old ones re-emerged) and caught fire, moving policing forward again? In exploring the answers we look at the role that Milwaukee and the MPD played in all of this.

Background: The Rise and Demise of Anglo Saxon Policing

During the mid-nineteenth century, police organizations as we know them were introduced into American cities. London devised and adopted this model in 1829; it made its way to Boston and New York during the 1840s, Milwaukee in 1854. The basic idea behind Anglo Saxon policing was that conspicuous uniformed officers would regularly patrol small geographical areas called beats, thereby preventing crime through their presence, by reducing opportunities for crime and persuading people to behave appropriately. Officers patrolled primarily on foot, although some use was made of horses. Criminal investigation and reactive detective work were marginalized in Anglo Saxon policing until the early twentieth century.

It is fair to say that technology would have a transformative impact on this mode of policing. First came the automobile. In the United States the introduction and acceptance of motorized police vehicles (motorcycles, wagons, and automobiles) occurred through a gradual process. The use of motorized patrol to respond rapidly to calls for service was recognized as early as 1909 when Louisville Chief J. H. Haager wrote: "Since almost every home is now provided with a telephone, the quick response of the automobile has resulted in much good and general satisfaction to our people."[14] As early as 1910, police began using motorized patrol wagons to transfer arrestees to jail and jailed felons to prison, and to provide ambulance service.[15] In Milwaukee, the first motorized squad car was used in 1913; by 1914, the MPD

---

14   J. H. Haager, "The Automobile as a Police Department Adjunct," *The Blue and the Brass*, (Gaithersburg, MD: International Association of Chiefs of Police, 1976), 174.

15   Marshal Farnan, "Use of Motor Vehicles by Police Departments," *The Blue and the Brass*, 179-181.

stopped using horse drawn wagons altogether.[16] In 1930, MPD Chief Jacob Laubenheimer installed one-way radios in patrol cars. The first radio dispatch was on Christmas Eve, 1930, when a man was shot on Sixteenth Street and National Avenue. In 1943, the MPD installed two-way radios in its patrol cars. (Until then, radio calls could be made to cars, but officers had to telephone in to communicate or to get more information.)[17]

Around the country, the ultimate impact of motorized vehicles equipped with radio communications would be to end foot patrol. By 1938, the Institute for Training in Municipal Administration (the original name of the International City Management Association—a national standard setting organization) declared: "A growing number of police administrators are coming to believe that most, if not all, foot patrols should be replaced by auto patrol."[18] By 1950, a nationwide switch to motorized patrol, at least conceptually, was complete. O. W. Wilson, in his classic text *Police Administration*, endorsed it wholeheartedly: "The automobile is undoubtedly the most effective and economical type of patrol when operated conspicuously by one man using superior patrol techniques."[19] The purported benefits were legion: police in cars could pursue fleeing offenders and respond to emergencies more rapidly; officers would be easier to supervise; cars could carry more police equipment; beats could be enlarged because cars could cover more territory; powerful cars would enhance the perceived power of police officers themselves; putting police in cars could help control corruption by removing police from intimate contacts with citizens; keeping police in cars, remote from citizen demand, would ensure their focus on departmental priorities—that is, serious crimes; police in cars could exploit the element of surprise by quickly arriving at some incident; and weather would not hamper patrol. Some police officials were so optimistic about the potential of cars that they predicted an end to street crime as it was then known.

---

16   Maralyn A. Wellauer-Lenius, *Milwaukee Police Department* (Charleston, SC: Arcadia Publishing, 2008), 31.

17   Ibid., p. 91.

18   *Municipal Police Administration* (Chicago, IL: The Institute for Training in Municipal Administration, 1938), 211.

19   O. W. Wilson, *Police Administration* (New York: McGraw-Hill Book Company, Inc., 1950), 98.

As use of cars became nearly universal, foot patrol was demeaned as an inefficient, antiquated means of patrolling. "Experts" from the International Association of Chiefs of Police, for example, ridiculed cities like Boston that persisted in using foot patrol into the 1960s, suggesting that police were doing criminals a favor with it. When used, foot patrol was often a punishment for officers who were out of favor or under some form of formal or informal discipline for misbehavior in the department. For example, after Milwaukee's police strike in 1971 Bob Kliesmet (who had to return to active duty from his PPA position due to the absence of a contract between the PPA and the city) was punished by being assigned to foot patrol on Capitol Drive from 20th to 27th Street.

By the 1960s, enthusiasm for motorized patrol became an operational rationale and the last word in police tactics. First, police believed that having a patrol car cruise randomly through neighborhoods, paying special attention to criminogenic hazards (such as bars or schools), would create a feeling of *police omnipresence*. This tactic, called preventive patrol, was thought to deter criminals, make citizens feel safe, create opportunities for police to intercept crimes in progress, and position police for the second major patrol tactic: rapid response to calls for service. Because having police cruise in cars was considered a crime prevention end in itself, it meant that officers would have more time available to respond to calls for service. The anticipated benefits of rapid response to calls for service were increased apprehension of criminals committing crimes (caught with the proverbial "smoking gun"), reduced citizen fear of crime and increased satisfaction with police, and deterrence of criminals fearing the imminent arrival of police. Response time, then, came to be considered one of the most significant indicators of police effectiveness.[20]

In retrospect, the mobilization of police into cars was a tactical shift that had greater impact than was ever imagined or anticipated. It is

---

20   A 1960s variation on preventive patrol was interception patrol, introduced by operations researchers and based on World War II anti-submarine warfare. The idea was to move patrol cars not only randomly but quickly through city streets with an eye to intercepting crimes in progress. In this model police success was defined as the number of "passings" of particular hazardous locations and response time. That preventive patrol, rapid response, and interception patrol would reduce crime was considered axiomatic.

not hard to argue that the genius of Anglo Saxon policing was its insertion of police into the heart of urban life. On the streets participating in urban society, police managed disputes, maintained order, assured strangers that they could move through cities unafraid and safe, and learned who the troublemakers were and kept an eye on them. The "significant others" in their daily work life were citizen users and residents of their beat. Of course police could be corrupted, they could abuse their authority, and they could (and did) discriminate against "undesirables." But, *at their best*, they were an integral part of neighborhood life. Arguably, this ended when police moved into cars.

Some advocates of mobilized patrol, especially O. W. Wilson, were not unaware of the tradeoffs as police shifted to patrol by cars. As Wilson noted: "[W]hile driving, the patrolman has less opportunity for observation and for contact with citizens than when on foot, and consequently he is less useful in furnishing information to citizens and in serving as the eyes and ears of the department."[21] Yet the apparent logic and intuitive sense of preventive patrol and rapid response to calls for service was so strong that it swept over policing. It was not only intuitively reasonable but internally coherent: riding in cars prevented crime and readied police for immediate response to calls; preventive patrol and rapid response "fit." As Milwaukee's Chief Jacob Laubenheimer said in 1938:

> When your phone call is received at police headquarters, squad cars are immediately directed to the scene by radio. No time is lost. A radio car will be at your doorstep shortly after you have hung up. If the information has been received in time, there is a very good chance to apprehend the person or persons committing the crime.[22]

O. W. Wilson's admonition about the potential losses from mobilizing police aside, American police charged headlong into motorized patrol as quickly as they could purchase cars, two-way radios, and ultimately computers to aid dispatch. Eventually computerized 911 systems were developed, and police marketed both 911 and its use. In some cities, such as Boston, district station telephone numbers were changed so citizens had to use 911 rather than district numbers.

---

21   Wilson, 99.

22   Jacob Laubenheimer, "The Citizen's Part in Crime Prevention," memo for the Milwaukee Police Department, 1938, 1-2.

Not fully appreciated, however, were the costs of abandoning foot patrol. In fact, we wind up with a classical example of the unintended consequences of purposive social action. Moving police into cars constituted a basic shift in the governing paradigm of policing. Until police were put into cars they had been primarily a preventive, proactive force. Once in cars, they became reactive—responding after the fact to incidents. The "significant others" of officers were no longer residents or users of beats, they were police partners and radio contacts—all of which created an isolated police culture. By avoiding neighborhood familiarity, police contacts with citizens were limited to troubled and troublesome people. Policing style became remote and "professional"—as television's Sergeant Friday put it: "Just the facts ma-am...." Protected in cars, police were freer to use a confrontational style with citizens, with little fear of consequences. Put succinctly, *tactics drove strategy rather than strategy driving tactics.*

Another Model of Policing

I recall an incident during the summer of 1968, a year after Milwaukee's riot, that exemplified an old—and what would become new—model of policing. The Commandos had obtained funds to administer a summer work program for youths; I worked with them to provide administrative assistance. We were about a week into the program and had established a pattern: each morning the Commandos would convene youths in an unused parking lot on Green Bay Avenue—a major thoroughfare lined with stores, many abandoned but a fair number still in operation. There, assignments would be made and groups, each led by one of the Commandos, would go off to their work assignments. We were in the parking lot for no more than half an hour.

One day, a police car with two officers pulled into the parking lot as we were setting up the teams and making assignments. The officers did not get out of the car. Instead, they rolled down the windows and ordered: "Get these kids out of this parking lot." The Commandos, spread over the area with the teams, started to converge on the police car. One of the Commandos tried to explain to the officers why they were there. The officers cut him off: "We don't care why you're here, get them out of here." An argument started. As more youths moved in the direction of the police car, the driver suddenly put his patrol car in reverse, backed out of the lot, and yelled that they would be back with help.

The Commandos, at this stage no strangers to confrontations (in contrast to me), went back to their business of getting the teams out for work. About fifteen minutes later a police car pulled up and parked across the street. A sergeant, probably about fifty and slightly over-weight, got out of his car, looked at what was going on, took off his hat and put it back in the police car, and then slowly crossed the street and entered the parking lot. Several of the Commandos, obviously old-er and bigger than the kids, were gathered together and the sergeant approached them and said "What's up?" Explanations of the program followed. After listening, the sergeant explained that the station had received several calls from the few remaining Green Bay Avenue mer-chants expressing concern about what their customers would think. The sergeant expressed both awareness of the value of what the Commandos were trying to do and concern for the remaining mer-chants who were having a tough time surviving. The sergeant won-dered if the daily gathering could take place somewhere else—perhaps a schoolyard nearby. The Commandos agreed that this presented no problem. The parley ended with the Commandos complaining about the attitudes of the two officers who had come earlier. The sergeant assured them not to worry now that he knew what was going on. They would not be back.

This event occurred several years before I became involved in police operations. (I started serious observations of police in Dallas in 1971.) Although it did not really deal with foot patrol, it has stayed with me as an example of differences in police style that are linked to automo-biles. The two officers were young and inexperienced. They were prod-ucts of the motorized patrol generation, without any real foot patrol or neighborhood experience. I suspect that they received a dispatch to what was perceived of as an incident: a gang of black youths congre-gating in a public space. Their expectation was that they had to break it up and they approached the situation with considerable apprehen-sion. They stayed in their cars, likely as a result of their anxiety about the circumstances. (Commandos were pretty impressive guys with a reputation for standing their ground.) Their confrontational approach evoked the very response they feared: resistance. Fortunately they re-treated, but with a promise to return with more force. The sergeant, on the other hand, both literally and figuratively disarmed himself by parking his car, getting out, taking off his hat, walking slowly, and politely asking what was going on. His casual approach was calculated to keep things calm. He deliberately made himself vulnerable, sending a message with his policing style that he was there to find out what was going on and to keep the peace. He recognized that there was a problem: the gathering of youths might scare off patrons of local stores. Likely he immediately spotted that this was not merely a random gathering but a purposeful meeting. He approached those who appeared to be the leaders and made an inquiry. The sergeant solved a problem and did it peacefully.

It was in this context that a new generation of police leaders was emerging that, rather than denying the failure of policing's autocentric strategy, took on the challenge of rethinking policing and its role in a democratic society. These leaders partnered with researchers and academics: scholars and consultants like Herman Goldstein, Robert Wasserman, Larry Sherman, Tony Pate, Mary Ann Wycoff, and many others became regulars in a police culture that up until a few years earlier had ignored and spurned them. These same police leaders understood that something had gone seriously wrong in the relationship between minorities, indeed all citizens, and police, and acknowledging that community relations was insufficient, moved to develop tactics that would be more readily acceptable in neighborhoods and communities. Finally, they acknowledged the failure of the then-current range of police tactics to prevent or control crime, and increasingly understood that police alone could not "own" the crime problem. They needed community partners. Out of all of this, community policing emerged—a strategy at first inchoate and without focus, but by the mid-1990s was internally cohesive and externally coherent.[23]

---

23   I would quickly add here that I am not suggesting that cars should not be used in policing or that calls for service should not be responded to promptly. Cars will continue to be used but riding around in cars, the dominant police activity during the 1950s to the 1970s, as an *end in itself*, will no longer be seen as a viable police tactic. Police will use cars to get to places where they can do police work—solve problems, maintain order. Likewise, police will always respond promptly to emergency calls, but the idea that they can respond to all calls immediately is not and has not been a feasible police tactic.

Milwaukee, which had been on the leading edge of police innovation for the first two-thirds of the twentieth century, quite simply was out of this picture. Starting with Chief Ziarnik and running through Chiefs Arreola, Jones, and Hegerty, Breier's legacy—an empowered union, professional isolation, and a dominant detective culture—in one form or another would frustrate chiefs' attempts to move the MPD into a preventive, community model of policing. Clearly the problems that occur in almost every organization—unsuspected crises in the organization's environment, inept or corrupt performance, technology failures—were to hinder progress by these chiefs as well. Nonetheless, the Breier shadow would affect the MPD until the twenty-first century.

CHAPTER FIVE

COMMUNITY POLICING:
EARLY EFFORTS, 1988–2007

By 1984, the year of Breier's resignation as Milwaukee's chief, police throughout the country were in a quandary. The certainties of mid-twentieth century policing were eroding. The riots of the 1960s might have receded in the memories of many officers and be "ancient history" to a new generation hired during the 1970s, but the Miami riot of 1980 in which fifteen people were killed and close to 200 injured renewed police awareness of ongoing volatility in the police-African American relationship. And still, police seemed helpless in the face of inexorable rises in crime; none of their tactics appeared effective. Nevertheless, during this decade major changes actually began to appear in American policing, arising in part from research findings and in part from on-the-ground attempts by police themselves to reach out to citizens and listen to their concerns. Quality of life issues, crime prevention, and even the resumption of foot patrol moved to the forefront of policing agendas. These were the early days of community policing—not accepted without dissension and subject to pushback from many who fought it, but still the movement had begun.

From the early 1980s forward, leading police executives ranging from Benjamin Ward and Lee Brown in New York City to Willie Williams and Bernard Parks in Los Angeles to Phillip Arreola, Arthur Jones, and Nanette Hegerty in Milwaukee struggled to implement community policing, a basic shift in policing's paradigm: from organizational centralization to decentralization; from after-the-fact responding to crime, disorder, and fear to preventing them in the first place; from organizational isolation to collaboration in problem solving; and from performance metrics based upon response time and clearances (crimes officially solved) to those reflecting the absence of crime, disorder, and fear. All these police leaders believed that the future of American policing lay in community policing; all worked mightily to implement it; yet all largely failed.

The challenges they faced were formidable. Conventional wisdom had it that response time to calls for service was a primary indicator of quality policing. Over the years unions had successfully bargained for work rules that severely limited a chief's ability to assign and promote officers. Mid-managers' traditional ways of running things tended to limit innovation. Civil service controlled recruitment and promotional procedures. Finally, powerful, internal interest groups such as special units and detectives resisted attempts to change how they operated. As a result, most chiefs and academics believed that implementing community policing in any department would take somewhere between five and ten years. Yet few chiefs in American cities lasted that long in office.[1] Union leaders often smirk when a new chief is sworn in because they expect to outlast him or her. Indeed it may take a chief a year to put together an effective administrative team. In many cities with strong civil service orientations, new chiefs must accept the command staff as it exists, waiting for some members to retire before replacing them—and even then the ability of chiefs to pick their immediate staff may be severely restricted. Many mid-managers enjoy civil service protection and simply decide to outwait the chief. New chiefs often wipe out the innovations implemented by their predecessors and install their own "flavor of the day." Chiefs selected from inside a department can be so beholden to internal personnel or departments (such as criminal investigators) that they cannot make the changes they would like.

Despite all of this, American policing went through dramatic changes during the 1990s as departments adopted community policing. In the process, police in the United States came to lead the world in crime prevention, and pulled other criminal justice agencies (prosecutors, courts, and corrections) along with them towards a community model. Police clearly contributed to widely recognized innovations in American urban governance. A number of large cities were prominent for their contributions to the new paradigm that reshaped American policing: during the 1970s, Kansas City, Missouri, for its research

---

1   The widely held view is that the average tenure of chiefs is between three and four years. See Fred W. Rainguet and Mary Dodge, "The Problems of Police Chiefs: An Examination of the Issues in Tenure and Turnover," *Police Quarterly* 4, no. 3 (September 2001): 268-288.

on preventive patrol and response time, and Cincinnati for research on team policing; during the 1980s, Minneapolis for research on domestic violence and "hot spots" of crime, Newark and Flint for foot patrol research, and St. Paul for bridging between team and community policing; and during the 1990s, Boston for gang control and New York City for compstat and its breakthrough in crime prevention and order maintenance. Many other cities and issues could be named. In Wisconsin, Madison became known as one of America's most innovative police departments as it experimented with community policing. For the most part Milwaukee remained in the backwaters of this movement.

Milwaukee certainly experienced the push and pull of old and new paradigms in policing after Harold Breier left office, with a number of chiefs who were more or less innovative. No longer at the forefront of American policing, the MPD was feeling its way through the administrations of four chiefs: Robert Ziarnik (1984-1989), Philip Arreola (1989-1996), Arthur Jones (1996-2003), and Nannette Hegerty (2003-2007). All took steps towards community policing, yet throughout this two-decade plus period (1984-2007), the MPD remained deeply committed to rapid response to 911 calls as *the* police metric and to a detective-oriented model of policing. In this chapter we follow the progression of their attempts to implement community policing in Milwaukee—attempts that largely failed.

THE STATE OF POLICING IN THE EARLY 1980S

For many, the assumption that police could do little but respond after a crime occurred was not surprising. At the time, the dominant idea in crime prevention held that crime was the result of poverty, racism, and social injustice, and thus it could only be prevented when massive social change rectified these problems. This view, advanced by many academics and some police leaders as well as President Johnson's prestigious crime commission, sidelined police in the development of crime prevention policy. They could respond, but their role in crime prevention was trivialized and reduced to instructing citizens about locks and security systems, prudent street behavior, locking cars, and not leaving valuables in view.

As a researcher I was as perplexed as anyone. I firmly believed that police could and should be able to do something about crime, but had no idea how this could be accomplished. Adding to my bewilderment was the fact that politicians and citizens in many communities continued to demand foot patrols despite the opposition of chiefs of police. For the vast majority of chiefs, foot patrol was at best a nostalgic hearkening back to the "good old days" of small communities and low levels of crime, but viewed largely as a waste of time in an increasingly urbanized, motorized, and suburbanized world. I had no real basis for doubting this, but still was intrigued by persistent citizen demand. Despite the police view of foot patrol and the accepted norm that politicians should keep their hands off police policies and practices, many politicians forced it on police departments. In Boston while Mayor Kevin White was in office from 1968 to 1984, foot patrol was reestablished in crucial areas with great fanfare virtually every time he ran for mayor (only to be withdrawn when the political season was over). Likewise in New Jersey, under the leadership of Governor William Cahill, foot patrol was forced on cities through the 1973 Safe and Clean Neighborhoods Act: if a city wanted the "clean" money (funds to clean up decrepit neighborhoods), it had to take the "safe" money (funds for foot patrol) as well—usually over the objection of chiefs of police.

It was New Jersey's Safe and Clean Neighborhood Act that gave me the opportunity to conduct an experiment on foot patrol during the late 1970s. At the time Patrick V. Murphy, former commissioner of the NYPD, was president of the Police Foundation. New Jersey Attorney General William Hyland was under pressure from local chiefs of police to allow cities to use the "safe" money to do "real" policing—in other words to increase their capacity to patrol in cars and rapidly respond to calls for service. Hyland asked Murphy for help in deciding how he should position himself on this issue. After sending in several consultants who produced unsatisfactory results, Murphy asked me to spend time in New Jersey observing and forming impressions about foot patrol. Consequently, along with my colleague, Tony Pate, I worked many afternoons and evenings in city after city, walking with foot patrol officers. I was uncertain about foot patrol's value. Although I sensed that something important was going on, I could not figure out what it was. There were several things I did note: foot patrol officers knew a lot of people by name (officers often introduced me to citizens); several merchants said to me "If foot patrol goes, I go" (meaning they would close up their shops if foot patrol ended); and I did not meet a citizen who was unenthusiastic about having a police officer walk in his or her neighborhood. As a result I suggested to Murphy that we conduct an experiment similar to the Kansas City study, this time adding and suspending foot patrol in neighborhoods.[2] My colleagues and I conducted the foot patrol experiment in Newark during 1978 and 1979, at about the same time that Michigan State University Professor Robert Trojanowicz was undertaking similar research in Flint, Michigan. Our findings were published about six months apart and they were remarkably similar: fear of crime declined in neighborhoods with foot patrol; fear of crime increased when foot patrol was withdrawn. Citizen satisfaction with police increased with foot patrol, yet decreased when foot patrol was withdrawn. Greater appreciation of citizens by police was felt among foot patrol officers than by officers in cars (in spite of the fact that during the Newark experiment most foot patrol beats were in African-American neighborhoods and almost all of the police were white). Although Trojanowicz found small but significant decreases in street crimes with foot patrol in Flint, we did not see this in Newark.[3]

Following the studies, many of us in police research were relieved that finally we could put some positive research findings on the table for police: both fear of crime and citizen satisfaction with police responded to foot patrol. And police attitudes toward citizens also improved with foot patrol. Still, this left police without much to go on and it raised as many questions as it answered. Putting aside the issue of reducing crime itself, was reducing *fear of crime* a legitimate police function? Was it possible that police attempts to reduce citizen fear of crime might succeed, yet inadvertently encourage citizens to behave in ways that increased their exposure to victimization?

These questions, in fact most of the questions asked by police researchers up to this period, were premised upon a particular view of the respective roles of citizens and police. Citizens were expected to detect crime and other problems and report them to police; police, in turn, were supposed to make it easy for citizens to mobilize them

---

2   George L. Kelling et al., *The Kansas City Preventive Patrol Experiment* (Washinton, D.C.: Police Foundation, 1975).

3   In retrospect, my belief is that the difference resulted from how the two experiments were conducted. In Flint, foot patrol was integrated into the overall tactical approach of the Flint Police Department. No such integration was attempted in Newark; officers there were pretty much isolated from their operational peers and only had occasional casual contacts.

to respond. In keeping with these premises, police created elaborate computer-based 911 (emergency call) systems, distributed police throughout the city using algorithms that would shorten the time it took them to respond to citizen calls, and provided patrolling officers with high-powered police vehicles. Within this framework, if crime increased police turned to options such as reducing the size of police beats, increasing the speed of patrol cars, adding more patrol cars, shortening the time spent handling citizen calls for service, prioritizing calls and not responding to some, and increasing the number of patrol car "passings" of "hazards," that is, criminogenic locations such as taverns, schools, or other such places considered troublesome. Indeed, during the late 1960s and early 1970s the first generation of researchers—using techniques developed during World War II anti-submarine warfare—helped police do just these things: in other words, to do better and faster that which police were already doing, regardless of the impact.

Contemporary readers may find this perplexing, but the premise that citizens observe and police respond, and its operational implications, had been gospel from the 1940s on. All of us were in this conceptual box and could not see out. Both preventive patrol by automobile and rapid response to calls for service were so intuitively reasonable that there seemed almost no other way to think about policing. The question confronting us all was: if patrolling in cars and responding quickly to calls did not impact crime, what would? Slowly, some started to question the assumptions that citizens should be passive in the face of crime and that police could do little more than respond after a crime was committed. Could community action prevent crime? What about neighborhood improvement, or building and landscaping design? Maintaining order? What role did commerce and private security play? Many more such questions were raised.

MILWAUKEE: THE BEGINNING MOVES TO COMMUNITY POLICING

Concerns about the ability of police to control crime and the role of the community were clearly on the minds of Milwaukee's political leaders early in the 1980s. In April of 1984, four months before Breier resigned, the Common Council ordered the Fire and Police Commission to create a crime prevention program in the MPD. Despite this move by the Common Council and its enthusiastic endorsement by community groups, the MPD was ill equipped to retool its strategy. Chief Breier had been vociferously disdainful of any community efforts. As far as he was concerned, civilians neither had anything to say of value about police nor should they have had any expectation that police should be accountable to them. By this time a whole generation of police had been recruited, trained, and promoted in accord with Breier's views of police and community. Notwithstanding his popularity with a segment of Milwaukeeans and the unwillingness of political and community leaders to directly "take him on" while he was chief, the Common Council's action made it clear that even while Breier was still in office his influence and ability to control the crime control agenda in Milwaukee was waning.

How much the Common Council's action affected Breier's decision to resign four months later is unknown. When these actions combined with state action to give more power over policy to the Fire and Police Commission (both the state legislature and the Common Council made their moves in April of 1984), however, a new world of community demands and changes in policing itself was closing in on Breier. Yet when faced with the Common Council's resolution to create a crime prevention unit, Breier appeared simply to ignore it. Not until his successor, Chief Robert Ziarnik created the Crime Prevention Unit in January of 1985 and placed it in the police academy did the MPD respond to the Common Council's resolution.

Chief Ziarnik was widely considered a transitional chief. According to then-Fire and Police Commissioner Robert San Fellipo, the Commission wrestled with how to replace Breier.[4] Commission members wanted a reformer with a new vision of policing, but were uncertain just what chance such a reformer would have in a department so dominated in the immediate past by Breier. Ultimately the Commission and Mayor Maier decided to go with someone they considered a transitional chief, Robert J. Ziarnik, an insider who many hoped could lay the groundwork for a future strong reformer.

Chief Ziarnik had retired from the MPD in 1983, after having served over thirty years. He was considered personally close to Breier and as assistant chief had been Breier's number-two person. Responses in the community to Ziarnik's appointment were mixed. Black leaders were either cautious or skeptical: the head of Milwaukee's NAACP,

4   Robert San Fellipo, interview by George Kelling, August 5, 2011.

Christine Belnavis commented: "Since Ziarnik was chief Breier's right-hand man, I don't think there will be any drastic changes in the police department." Arthur Jones, president of the MPD's League of Martin (the black officers' association), was non-committal, indicating he did not know Ziarnik; the Milwaukee Police Association's president, Bill Krueger, was supportive, believing Ziarnik could run the department.[5]

In fact Ziarnik proved to be more than a transitional or "caretaker" chief. He created the Crime Prevention Unit; involved the MPD in research that replicated the Minneapolis Domestic Violence Experiment (an experiment in how police should best respond to domestic violence); reached out to the community in meetings; began the computerization of the department, especially computer-aided dispatch; instituted officer use of bulletproof vests; and implemented a new deployment plan that included foot patrol. Ziarnik created the Neighborhood Foot Patrol Program in 1988 with a strong statement that incorporated most of the thinking on community policing at the time. Order Number 9995 also included a mission statement positing improvement in the quality of life in neighborhoods as a major goal of the MPD, encouraged citizen participation in crime prevention, urged police to involve other agencies in problem solving, ordered officers to contact and counsel victims, and recognized that the problems with which officers dealt would vary from beat to beat. All these were, and are, elements of community policing.[6]

Generally, as the foot patrol program was instituted it was comprised of assigning three to five officers for full-time foot patrol per district, and a park and walk program for routine patrol by officers in cars. In the park and walk program a senior officer who remained in the car was paired with a junior officer who was supposed to walk for one to four hours. Generally the park and walk program came to be known, both during Ziarnik's and subsequent administrations, as the "farce and walk" program because so few officers really spent the allocated time on foot patrol.[7] Moreover as current MPD Assistant Chief

---

5   *Milwaukee Sentinel*, September 7, 1984, p. 14.

6   Order No. 9995, Milwaukee Police Department, December 16, 1988.

7   Based on my experience in many cities, this was not unusual. Police during the early stages of community policing simply did not want to get out of their cars, regardless of the city.

James Harpole notes, the foot patrol program as envisioned was quite different from the program as executed:

> Although I enjoyed the job as a foot patrol officer assigned to the Neighborhood Foot Patrol program, I found it frustrating because we were frequently removed from our foot beats to take assignments in radio cars. I would frequently find myself in a position where I had a block watch meeting scheduled and a supervisor, who did not understand the program, would pull me off the foot beat to take assignments. This was most challenging because oftentimes there was a house full of people waiting to hear from me and I would have to cancel at the last minute. The foot officers also gave presentations to schools, community centers, senior centers, etc. and the same problem would arise with schedule presentations and last minute cancellations. When I could actually walk the beat and engage the community it was a great job. I decided to go back on squad patrol because the frequent cancelations diminished the credibility of the program and the officers assigned.[8]

Part of the problem was that at about the same time Chief Ziarnik was attempting to implement a substantial foot patrol program, Milwaukee, like cities throughout the country, was also developing and implementing a computer-based 911 system. Thus computer-aided dispatch (perhaps the "jewel in the crown" of the 1940s-1970s police reform movement emphasizing reactive law enforcement) came to the fore in the 1980s and overlapped with the beginning stages of community policing (promoting proactive crime prevention). In such circumstances, Harpole's experiences are not hard to understand: the real business of the MPD—the leading edge of policing for those who had been recruited, hired, and promoted by Breier—was responding to calls for service (referred to as "hitches" in Milwaukee). In such a world, foot patrol was a luxury that could be indulged when 911 demand was low, but actually in the MPD it was used as a reserve personnel pool to be drawn upon whenever "important" problems developed. Defining police work as responding to calls for service was not only driven administratively; it became part of the police culture. As Assistant Chief Harpole notes:

> I remember cops thinking the program was soft on crimes and that the officers assigned were not doing "real" police work.

---

8   Assistant Chief James Harpole, Milwaukee Police Department, communication with George Kelling, July 19, 2013.

Neighborhood Foot Patrol officers had to frequently put up with sarcastic comments from other cops who bragged about how hard they worked and all the arrests they made, while Neighborhood Foot Patrol officers, in their opinion, did not do real police work.[9]

None of these issues was unique to Milwaukee. And if Ziarnik was a transitional chief, it was not in the sense that Milwaukee's leaders anticipated. Despite his closeness to Breier, Ziarnik was attempting to move Milwaukee into the mainstream of police thinking and development. Nevertheless, three issues—seat belts, bulletproof vests, and redeployment—became sources of intense conflict among Ziarnik and the police union, some members of Milwaukee's Common Council, and the Fire and Police Commission.[10] After publicly threatening to resign several times, Ziarnik finally did so in anger on April 21, 1989.

THE 1990S AND EARLY TWENTY-FIRST CENTURY: MPD'S TROUBLED TIMES

Although Henry Maier was mayor when Chief Ziarnik was appointed, Ziarnik completed his term under Mayor John Norquist. After Ziarnik three other chiefs served during Norquist's time in office from 1988 to 2004: Phillip Arreola (1989-1996), Arthur Jones (1996-2003), and Nannette Hegerty (2003-2007). Even though Norquist resigned from office as the result of a scandal in 2004, his sixteen years as mayor made him, at the time, one of the country's longest serving major city mayors. Often labeled a "fiscally conservative socialist," Norquist was also a social liberal. He articulated his vision of city life in a book, *The Wealth of Cities*. Norquist was a staunch advocate of public transportation and school choice. Both his support for school choice and attempts to reduce the power of the Milwaukee Police Association gained him the animosity of public sector unions. Nonetheless, while regularly reducing property taxes he rejected the financial reliance of cities on the federal government, which he called "tin cup federalism."[11] When elected, Norquist was dismayed that under Mayor Maier not

9   Assistant Chief James Harpole, communication to George Kelling, July 20, 2013.

10   See, for example, "Council Panel Demands Data on Patrols," *Milwaukee Journal*, June 10, 1987.

11   Charles Mahtesian, "Urban Theorist As Mayor: Secrets of a 'fiscally conservative socialist,'" *Governing: The States and Localities*, 1998, accessed

a single city department had been headed by a minority and he took steps to remedy the situation: the first chief to serve during Norquist's administration was an Hispanic male (Arreola), the second an African American male (Jones), and the third a white woman (Hegerty).

Although each chief was eligible for two terms, none served beyond his or her first term: Arreola and Jones each served seven years and was not reappointed; Hegerty, served four years but then resigned.[12] The challenge facing all three was to move the MPD away from reactive, after-the-fact law enforcement tactics to the preventive tactics fundamental to community policing. Given Milwaukee's recent history this would be a formidable task. Clearly Ziarnik had laid some of the groundwork with his community and foot patrol programs, even though the extent to which these filtered down through mid-management and sergeants was questionable: community policing primarily augmented the mid-century police tactics of patrolling in cars and responding to calls. Arguably Philip Arreola was the first Milwaukee chief who really understood and was a staunch advocate of community policing, not merely as an add-on tactic but as an overall strategy with implications ranging from how police related to and were allocated throughout the community to the nature and development of police priorities to how police were recruited, hired, trained, and supervised, and to how police gained and maintained their legitimacy in the community.

But Arreola was stymied from the outset. First, as a former Detroit commander and Port Huron, Michigan, chief, he was Milwaukee's first chief of police to be hired from outside the department, a move bitterly opposed by the Milwaukee Police Association. As far as most police officers were concerned this was a slap in the face by the Fire and Police Commission and Mayor Norquist. For them, the MPD had plenty of talent so there was no need to even consider an outsider. Second and equally profound, the vast majority of police officers— and this was not just a Milwaukee phenomenon—wanted nothing to do with community policing. While community policing might

November 24, 2014, http://www.governing.com/poy/john-norquist.html.

12   Initially after Breier, a term of seven years was set with an option of being appointed to a second term. Later the term was set at four years, also with an option of a second term. This explains why Hegerty only served four years.

have been popular with politicians and many chiefs, for line officers it was "soft" policing, more akin to dreaded social work than the "tough" law enforcement to which they were accustomed. Few chiefs were so openly disdainful of community policing as was Breier. And although Ziarnik's opposition had softened during his administration, still he could not be called an advocate of community policing either conceptually or in reality. On the other hand, from the beginning Arreola was an open and determined supporter of community policing, at least as it was conceived during the 1980s into the 1990s.

Finally, Chief Arreola's personal and administrative styles were completely different from and alien to the authoritarian approaches that had dominated the MPD for over twenty-five years. Arreola was open, friendly, wanted to discuss ideas, and given to searching for consensus rather than merely handing down orders. For many including union leaders, this way of operating represented a weakness rather than the transformational leadership for which he had been hired. The MPD was ill-prepared for such an administrative style. The deal that Breier had struck with his officers—to protect them from any outside control or influence—gave rise to an aggressive, "kick ass and take names" policing style that continued, but now under sergeants and command staff who knew nothing other than an authoritarian approach. Consequently in the view of many current MPD leaders departmental discipline and accountability worsened, especially during the early years of Arreola's administration.

In addition to these three bases of resistance against him—for being the first outside chief, an advocate of community policing, and for his administrative style—Arreola also faced two huge challenges that lay outside of his control, at least during their early stages: the "crack" epidemic and the Jeffrey Dahmer case. The crack epidemic hit Milwaukee hard. Crack, made from cocaine powder, was easy to produce, cheap, and highly addictive. Although it hit other areas of the country by the early 1980s, crack entered Milwaukee only during the late 1980s at about the same time Arreola assumed leadership of the MPD. According to current police executives Milwaukee had never seen anything like it.[13] Where before the call for service load had been manageable, after crack it was overwhelming—officers went "from hitch to hitch." Crime soared: murders almost doubled from eighty-six in 1988 (Chief Ziarnik's last full year) to 168 in 1991 (Chief Arreola's

13   MPD leadership, focus group by George Kelling, December 12, 2012.

second full year), an increase of over 95 percent. Other factors aside, Arreola inherited a crime epidemic for which many, including Mayor Norquist, were not satisfied with the MPD's response.

Adding to Arreola's management and crime woes was the Jeffrey Dahmer affair. On July 22, 1991, approximately two years after Arreola's appointment, Jeffrey Dahmer was arrested after committing seventeen murders. A handcuffed potential victim of Dahmer had escaped and flagged down a passing patrol car. Upon investigating the incident, police officers discovered the grisly remains of multiple homicides. At the time, Dahmer was on probation for a series of minor sexual offenses and had had multiple contacts with the criminal justice system. As the early investigation proceeded it turned out that three MPD police officers had had contact with Dahmer and one of his victims two months prior to Dahmer's arrest: a fourteen year old Laotian boy, Konerak Sinthasomphone. On May 27, 1991, local residents discovered Sinthasomphone wandering naked and disoriented on the street during the early morning hours. Witnesses to the encounter among the boy, Dahmer, and police charged that police ignored their pleas that something was seriously wrong and required strong police action. The three police officers ultimately accepted Dahmer's claim that this was a quarrel between two consenting adult lovers and allowed Dahmer to lead Sinthasomphone back to his apartment. Dahmer killed him shortly thereafter. As this encounter became known, a political firestorm erupted.

As Anne E. Schwartz indicated in her book, *The Man Who Could Not Kill Enough: The Secret Murders of Milwaukee's Jeffrey Dahmer*, the MPD was criticized from every direction: African Americans alleged ongoing racism in the MPD (the majority of the victims were black); Laotians charged that police would have investigated the matter far more thoroughly had the boy been white; and gays claimed that police homophobia explained how police handled the first Dahmer encounter.[14] The case attracted national attention, with Jesse Jackson coming to Milwaukee to lead a protest involving over a thousand persons. Adding to the picture, all of this occurred within the national context

---

14   Anne E. Schwartz, *The Man Who Could Not Kill Enough: The Secret Murders of Milwaukee's Jeffrey Dahmer* (New York: Carol Publishing Group, 1992), 98. This account was written by a reporter who managed to gain access both to the murder scene during the early minutes and hours of the police investigation, and to police sources throughout the investigation.

of the beating of Rodney King by Los Angeles police and the ensuing fear of violence and riots. During August and September, 1991, in quick succession, Arreola suspended the three officers; the Milwaukee Police Association sponsored a vote in which over 90 percent of its 1339 members voted no-confidence in the chief and over 50 percent rated his performance as poor;[15] and Arreola fired two of the three officers, at least in part to assuage community indignation and fear of violence and rioting. Ultimately courts overturned the firing: one of the two officers went to work in another local police department while the other remained in the MPD and ultimately was elected president of the Milwaukee Police Association. Dahmer was convicted, imprisoned, and killed in prison by another inmate.

Apart from the questions as to whether Arreola's judgments were reasonable, the validity of the complaints against individual officers or the department as a whole, or the extent to which race or homophobia were critical issues in the entire affair, the overall accumulation of these factors along with the crack epidemic and crime surge doomed Arreola's administration. Even a University of Wisconsin-Milwaukee newspaper, the *University of Wisconsin-Milwaukee Times*, regularly counted the days since Chief Arreola "*should have*" resigned.[16]

In the midst of all of this Mayor Norquist created the Citizen Commission on Police–Community Relations on August 6, 1991 to examine "the Milwaukee Police Department's performance of service to the public, particularly in the areas of responsiveness and sensitivity to diversity within the community." As the Commission's October 15 report notes:

> The Citizen Commission was created in response to public expression of dissatisfaction with Police Department service. Residents complained of slow response time, racist and homophobic attitudes, and a general lack of respect from police officers. These claims are not new; in 1981, a study of community attitudes conducted for the Milwaukee Fire and Police Commission found the same complaints.[17]

15 Ibid., 170. See also "Police Officers in Milwaukee Vote No Confidence in Chief," *New York Times*, August 8, 1991.

16 Schwartz, 171.

17 "A Report to Mayor John O. Norquist and the Board of Fire and Police Commission," The Mayor's Citizen Commission on Police-Community Relations, October 15, 1991, p. ii.

The Commission also quoted from, and went on to emphasize, a 1988 report by Carroll Buracker & Associates:

> "The Department has not routinely employed response time data as a basis for determining staffing needs. This is atypical in law enforcement." Buracker recommended that the Department should establish a "calls for service" staffing model, that district squad areas should be based on workload [read calls for service] and be flexible by shift, and that the Department should analyze response times by priority in order to monitor patrol distribution and allocation.[18]

The work of the 1991 Citizen Commission was impressive. In two months it produced a report that, for the most part, reflected advanced thinking about policing and the changes taking place nationally. The Commisson's endorsement of community policing and the need to implement it rapidly, especially in light of the controversies about race that had plagued the MPD and the city itself, was persuasive.

Yet in one respect the report endorsed a police tactic that interfered with the adoption of community policing in Milwaukee until well into the twenty-first century, driving police priorities in other directions. By citing and endorsing the Carroll and Buracker & Associates recommendation that the MPD develop a "calls for service staffing model" rather than a community policing neighborhood staffing model, the Citizen Commission undermined its own recommendations. The conclusion of the Commission and the Buracker report contributed to the subsequent elevation of calls for MPD service to comprise Milwaukee's primary police workload, using response time as the principal indicator of police effectiveness, and constructing beats and precincts/districts on the basis of call for service workload. This approach was not unique to Milwaukee: calls for service and response time measures were conundrums for every police department then, and continue to be today. Response time has been touted as an indicator of police effectiveness for so long and is so intuitively reasonable that the slogan of "slow response time" has become the mantra for those dissatisfied with police service. Yet no evidence exists that rapid response to calls for service actually prevents crime, captures more "bad guys," protects citizens, or improves the quality of life in neighborhoods; in fact, as noted above in Chapter Two, research suggests that response time has little impact on crime or victimization. What overemphasis

18   Ibid., 12.

on response time does do, however, is to provide justification for those police who want to stay in cars and to keep officers in cars who want to get out to do police work. One way or the other it reduces the contacts that police have with citizens. Relative to this, policing has a telling nomenclature: police officers riding around in their cars doing nothing else are "in service;" police officers who are out of their cars dealing with citizens are "out of service." Organizational pressure in police departments is brought on officers to be "in service" waiting for the next call. This focus on response time turns police departments into emergency response law enforcement agencies rather than the crime prevention agencies they were originally conceived to be. Few chiefs have faced up to this inherent inconsistency as they develop police strategy and tactics.

Such issues aside, despite Arreola's desire for a second seven-year term as chief, Mayor Norquist and the Fire and Police Commission did not reappoint him. Arreola subsequently became the Chief of Police in Tacoma, Washington. Mayor Norquist and the Fire and Police Commission named Arthur Jones, an African American, Chief of Police on November 15, 1996. Jones was a controversial figure in the MPD long before he became Chief. Almost literally taking time off from demonstrating with Father Groppi and the Commandos to apply to become a police officer—in his words "policing was a good job with a decent salary and good benefits"—Jones joined the MPD in 1967. In that year, of the eighty-two appointments to the MPD six were African American. During the ten years prior to Jones joining the MPD (1958-1967), of the 865 persons appointed to the MPD, thirty-four were African American, two Hispanic, and none native American.[19] Confronted with what he and his African American colleagues perceived of as racial bias in recruitment, assignments, and promotions, Jones sought to overcome it both as an individual and organizationally throughout his career in the MPD. Alone, he confronted supervisors and mid-managers with his concerns about assignments: assigning black officers to foot rather than car patrol, limiting the assignment of black officers to districts with large African American populations, rigging the "acting" detective system to ensure that blacks could not become full fledged detectives. Early on Jones joined a group of African American officers who met informally to

---

19   Email communication from Fire and Police Commission researcher to
      George Kelling, December 4, 2012.

discuss what they perceived to be problems of the MPD: in 1974 this group became the League of Martin (LOM), taking its name from Martin Luther King. Jones was not only one of the original members but the LOM's president for fourteen years.

Considerable evidence existed that Jones' and the League of Martin's perceptions of serious internal and external problems regarding race in the MPD were well founded. For example, a 1981 survey by a consultant firm, DMT & S, found that African-American citizens believed that "officers use more force when restraining and arresting minority suspects" and "that the MPD treats minorities worse than whites." The survey also found:

> [S]ubstantial racial polarization within the MPD, with the majority of African American officers rating the relationship between themselves and the Department negatively, including dissatisfaction with promotional opportunities and assignment practices. At that time, there were no African American officers above the rank of sergeant, and few on special squads.

The report concluded: "the most important problem currently facing the Commission and the Department is the substantial alienation of a major portion of Black Milwaukeeans from the police department."[20]

In 1976 the League of Martin headed by Jones, along with the National Association for the Advancement of Colored People, brought legal action against the city. The result was a consent decree requiring that two out of every five new employees hired be African American, Hispanic, or Native American, and that one in five be a woman. It was within this context that Jones moved up within the department. In January of 1978 he became a detective; in 1987 he became a lieutenant of detectives; and in 1988 he was picked by newly elected Mayor John Norquist to head the mayor's security detail. In 1989 he became a captain, stayed for a while to head the security detail, and then in sequence headed District Seven (Milwaukee's large northwest high-crime district) and the special operations bureau. Finally in 1996 he was appointed MPD's first African American chief.

Although the relationships among the mayor, Fire and Police Commission, and Jones started out on a friendly and professional basis, they deteriorated throughout the Jones administration. While most crimes leveled off or decreased modestly during this era, homicides

---

20   Quoted in "A Report to Mayor John O. Norquist," 10. See n. 17 above.

reached all time highs. The Fire and Police Commission headed by Woody Welch and Mayor Norquist believed that plans for controlling homicides were inadequate, demanded that Jones take strong action, and created a community crime commission to make recommendations. Jones viewed this as inappropriate political interference with his prerogatives, motivated by racial bias. A bitter public dispute arose with Norquist and the Fire and Police Commission, and eventually the City Council became involved. Members of the Common Council asked Jones to take a leave of absence during the dispute, and the mayor and members of the Commission sought ways to dismiss Jones. Jones then filed a discrimination suit against the city with the federal Equal Employment Opportunity Commission. Ultimately, the complaint went nowhere, Jones finished his seven year term, was not reappointed, and Nannette Hegerty was appointed chief.

In retrospect, Jones was a strong believer in community policing and in a broken windows approach to controlling disorder and preventing crime. He fought his way to the top of the MPD during an era when both the city and MPD were racially polarized. As chief he worked to end abusive police tactics, control overtime, and advance computerization. He also oversaw the construction of a new District Three and Communications Center, an achievement of which he is justly proud. There is no doubt that as Jones fought his way to the top a lot of "games" were played even after he received promotions. For example, he was made to sit outside of the security office when as a lieutenant he was first assigned to the mayor's security detail.[21] Once he was chief, the police union was unrelenting in its opposition. For Jones this was a sign of their racism; for the union, this opposition was largely the result of Jones' aggressive micro-management of the department and his assignment of trivial complaints against officers to the Internal Affairs Bureau. Many, to this day, compare Jones' administrative practices as akin to Breier's: authoritarian and arbitrary, moving swiftly to discipline or investigate even the most minor offenses, such as being outside a police car without a hat. Detectives resented his requirement that they be first responders to crime scenes.[22] During Jones' admin-

21 Arthur Jones, interview by George Kelling, November 26, 2012.

22 Jones maintains that his intention was to increase the productivity of detectives by insisting that they regularly got out into neighborhoods and communities. In respects, such an approach has merit; however it presents at least two problems. First, it results in the underutilization of patrol

istration seventeen white officers sued him for "reverse discrimination" in his promotion practices. (The officers ultimately won their case, but only after Jones left office.) Finally, Milwaukee's Common Council, Fire and Police Commission, and mayor believed that Jones was underperforming as chief and was unwilling to take advice about alternative means of reducing violence. Chief Jones believed their criticism and opposition had its origins in racism and discrimination.[23]

Like Arreola, Jones wanted to be reappointed to a second term. Instead, the Fire and Police Commission and Mayor Norquist appointed Nannette Hegerty on November 18, 2006. Hegerty's administration is discussed above in Chapter One. In contrast to the two chiefs who preceded her, Hegerty enjoyed broad-based popularity and faced little real resistance either at her appointment or subsequently. Originally an MPD officer—Hegerty joined the MPD in 1976—she rose to the rank of captain. President William Clinton appointed her as the United States Marshal for the Eastern District of Wisconsin in 1994. Probably more than any of Milwaukee's previous chiefs (and for that matter most chiefs throughout the country), she aggressively restored discipline and penetrated the "blue curtain" that has often scandalized American policing (that is, the unwillingness of officers to come forward when their colleagues behave illegally or brutally).

Although Hegerty disciplined officers for a wide variety of crimes and offenses—she fired thirty-seven officers—it was her persistence in the Frank Jude case that especially caught attention.[24] On October 24, 2004, Frank Jude, a man of mixed race, was savagely beaten at a party by a group of off-duty police who accused him of stealing an officer's badge. Observers called police and when uniformed police arrived at the scene, they joined in the beating. Hegerty fired nine officers and

---

officers. Their job becomes merely responding to a call and then waiting for detectives to arrive. Second, it ignores the research into criminal investigation that has consistently demonstrated that the single most important factor in solving crimes is the preliminary investigation by patrol officers. These practices, however, were maintained through the Hegerty administration and still have some impact today.

23   For an interesting, largely sympathetic, account of Arthur Jones' career, see Jonathan Gramling, "And Still I Rise: The Story of Arthur Jones, Milwaukee's First Black Top Cop," *Capital City Hues*, June 13, 27, and July 11, 2007.

24   "Hegerty to Retire," *Milwaukee Journal Sentinel*, January 6, 2007.

disciplined three others. Despite aggressive prosecution by District Attorney E. Michael McCann, the officers' solidarity prevented a state court conviction. Federal prosecution of four officers for violation of civil rights followed, and three were convicted and imprisoned. Three other officers pled guilty and testified against the other officers. Hegerty's strong action sent a message both to the community and to Milwaukee police.

During the early post-Breier era then, Milwaukee and the MPD moved into unfamiliar territory in at least two dimensions: the evolution of community policing, and new relationships among Milwaukee's chief, mayor, commission, police union and Common Council. Regarding the new relationships, the rules of the game had changed. No longer did a chief have the autonomy, independence, and lack of accountability of Breier's and earlier administrations. The actions of the state legislature to set term limits for the MPD's chief and, along with the decisions of arbitrators to make rules, regulations, and policies negotiable, resulted in redefining the MPD's relationship to its political and social context. For good or ill, the Fire and Police Commission had gained considerable control over policy matters and the commission in turn was affected by mayoral and city council politics. One can argue that all—chief, mayor, commission, and council—were feeling their way in this unfamiliar new world. What if any influence each should have in determining patrol deployment, beat and district design, departmental or neighborhood priorities, or disciplinary matters were just a few policy areas of concern. The struggles over these issues were intense and ultimately led to the early resignation of Ziarnik, and to the one-term tenures of Arreola and Jones. Hegerty seemed to have learned the lesson: in the new world of political accountability, political and social skills had to be part of the portfolio of effective police leaders and managers.

At the same time, the new paradigm of community policing was overthrowing the reactive law enforcement model that had dominated policing during most of the twentieth century. While some of its features—such as improving the relationship with local citizens, especially minority communities—gained support, community policing as a whole remained in inchoate form until well into the twenty-first century throughout the country, with many questions not yet answered. If the next Milwaukee chief implemented community policing, s/he would face issues about its impact on departmental goals and organizational structure, on administrative processes such as recruitment and training, and on policing tactics. These critical issues, along with many others, were at the forefront in the police administration in Milwaukee.

CHAPTER SIX

A NEW DIRECTION: CHIEF ED FLYNN'S STRATEGY FOR DEVELOPING COMMUNITY POLICING AND PROBLEM SOLVING

Chief Edward Flynn assumed leadership of the Milwaukee Police Department in January 2009 with the explicit mission of implementing what he called "community-based, problem-oriented, data-driven" policing. For Flynn, the purpose of this form of policing was, and is, to create and support neighborhoods capable of sustaining civic life. Flynn is of the generation that came into policing during the 1970s when good policing meant responding to serious crime by riding around in cars responding to calls for service. He began as a foot patrol officer in Hillside, New Jersey, in 1971 and then joined the Jersey City Police Department in 1973, rising to the rank of inspector by 1988. Chief Flynn completed course work for a Ph.D. at the John Jay College of Criminal Justice in 1988, but did not go on to do a dissertation. He served as chief of police in Braintree and Chelsea, Massachusetts, and Arlington County, Virginia; was appointed Secretary of Public Safety for the State of Massachusetts in 2003; and then became commissioner of police in Springfield, Massachusetts, in 2006. In January 2008, he became Milwaukee's seventeenth police chief—only the second chief to come from outside the MPD.

I have known Chief Flynn since the early 1990s when he was a chief in Massachusetts. In the field of policing—and in my judgment as well—Flynn was generally seen as an up-and-coming leader in the business who would contribute substantively to its development.

Today he is considered extremely bright and articulate, although at times as somewhat loquacious and brash. His opinions are sought out by many in the policing world, particularly as a spokesperson for community policing.

This chapter chronicles the course undertaken by Chief Flynn to transform the MPD in pursuit of his vision of policing. One can take either of two positions regarding the credibility of this account: on the down side, some might say that my familiarity with Flynn biases my perspective so that I lack objectivity about the happenings under discussion and portray them in too positive a light. Alternatively, it can be argued that my familiarity with Flynn has given me uncommon access to the MPD, the changes being made, and Flynn's thinking, thereby allowing me to present a unique view of the MPD's evolution. Probably a little bit of both is true: while not completely neutral, I believe my familiarity with and proximity to important players, and the access afforded me allow for a rare perspective.

When I began working in Milwaukee in 2007, the MPD reminded me of two departments in which I had served as a consultant for substantial periods of time previously: the New York City Police Department of the early 1990s and the Los Angeles Police Department of the early 2000s. Each was estranged from its community, underperforming, and out of touch with latest developments in policing nationally. So too was the MPD. Yet also like New York City and Los Angeles, Milwaukee's Police Department was loaded with talented personnel who had joined the department over the years. These officers were often embedded in middle management. They had no investment in defending the tactics of the past. Many had become familiar with the latest criminal justice and police research in college; virtually all had had to study this research in preparation for promotional civil service exams. Many were impatient at the unwillingness of risk-averse senior MPD managers to move beyond outdated mid-twentieth century police thinking. Both the Jones and Hegerty administrations were long on discipline, but short on vision or urgency—response time and clearance rates simply did not comprise a vision of policing and its potential that could rally the new generation of officers or citizens. New York City detective Michael Toone summed up such circumstances in his own department under a past administration as "Plenty of supervision; no leadership."[1]

In other words, the MPD had a cadre of middle managers and young officers eager for change. This partially explains the acceptance that Wasserman and I met upon beginning our work in the MPD, but more importantly, the readiness of the department to accept and ultimately embrace an outside chief. Compared with Chief Arreola's reception—as the first chief from outside the department he was sandbagged from every direction—by the time Flynn was appointed many, if not the majority, of Milwaukee's police officers were ready to rid themselves of the past: to shake off the professional and organizational isolation, lack of urgency and vision, absence of leadership, and department's reputation for brutality; to once again be part of an organization striving for the leading edge of policing. Even the police union quietly accepted an outsider as chief.

A RUNNING START

Chief Flynn's first concern was to develop a sense of urgency about Milwaukee's violent crime problem within the MPD and build momentum toward achieving his vision. To these ends, he took immediate action on four fronts: first, articulating a vision of community policing to unify the department around a crime prevention strategy; second, achieving a series of quick wins that would allow him to identify talent inside the MPD, create a sense of urgency about solving problems, and gain community attention and involvement; third, improving the MPD's information technology so as to enhance its capacity to identify and address crime problems as well as maintain accountability; finally, gaining control over calls for service in order to provide officers more uncommitted time to be directly involved in problem solving.

A New Mission

From his first meeting with the command staff and on through attending early roll calls with line police officers, Chief Flynn focused on his vision of the core mission of the MPD: preventing crime, disorder, and fear, and sustaining civic life. Both these ends had to be achieved within the law and in collaboration with neighborhoods and

---

1   Michael Toone, personal conversation with George Kelling, March 28, 2014.

communities. Flynn's starting point for implementing this new mission lay in presenting a clear overarching organizational strategy—one that he hoped would not only reduce crime but also capture the enthusiasm and professional aspirations of line police officers, and mid-level and top executives alike. Moreover this strategy had to be articulated in ways that citizens would understand, and political and social elites endorse.

Every aspect of the MPD's functioning would be evaluated in terms of how it contributed to achieving this core mission, both internally (through its structure and organizational processes) and externally (by developing the MPD's relationship to neighborhoods and communities). Internally the issues that were addressed ranged from district and beat construction to tactics for addressing crime, disciplinary systems, the organizational structure of the MPD, and administrative systems and processes (such as recruitment and training). Every morning, the command staff would meet to discuss, on a district-by-district basis, neighborhood crime problems, departmental responses and capacities, early outcome indicators, as well as administrative issues such as controlling overtime—a decades long problem in Milwaukee. Externally the MPD would work with every sector of Milwaukee's social, business and political structure: neighborhood organizations, religious groups, business and commerce, and political and legislative entities including the mayor, Common Council, and the Fire and Police Commission.

Quick Wins in the Districts

Recognizing the value of quickly showing that the new MPD mission could lead to concrete achievements, Flynn instructed each of the seven district commanders to identify a problem in her/his district, develop plans to deal with it, identify working partners, meet with the community involved, implement the plans, and contact community representatives six weeks later to report on their progress. Flynn would attend both the community kickoffs and report meetings in each district. The purposes of the effort were to develop a sense of urgency in district commanders, to immediately focus the commanders on the MPD's core mission on a neighborhood-by-neighborhood basis, to establish accountability both within the MPD and to communities, and to develop confidence that commanders really could prevent crime, establish order, and reduce fear.

Most plans were quite ambitious. For example, District Three's plan, entitled the Historic Concordia/Wells Street Neighborhood Policing Plan, set multiple goals: to reduce disorder, crime (especially violent crime), and calls for service; to implement nuisance abatement activities; to build strong community relations, and enhance police credibility and community ownership of the plan. To accomplish these goals, District Three anticipated forming twenty working partnerships with groups and agencies ranging from the Milwaukee County District Attorney's office to local churches and businesses. The MPD and its partners would collaborate in at least twenty-three different sets of activities—from foot patrols to newsletters to focused targeting of repeat offenders—in all, a profusion of problems, partners, and methods.[2]

Despite what appeared to be overly ambitious goals and tactics in several districts, gains were made on several fronts. Post-project reports generally found modest reductions in key crimes. Commanders began to sense their dual accountability to the MPD and the community; they felt pride in what they did, and empowered to pursue problems freely as they saw fit. Unlike earlier times when the primary metrics of evaluation had been clearances and response time, if dispatch (response time) was mentioned in these efforts it was generally portrayed as an obstacle, as one District Three progress report noted: "Resources dedicated to this mission are...pulled by dispatchers for assignment to other areas of the district. ... Officers selected to perform park and walk duties ... have been denied the opportunity on several occasions by dispatch."[3]

Assessing the importance of the entire quick wins effort, Assistant Chief James Harpole (who was Commander of District Three) summarized:

> We had few restrictions placed on us and the ability to be creative and innovative was a motivator for the district teams. I remember pulling my team together after the quick win initiative was given to us, they were so excited that we were going to do this; until this point the patrol staff felt that chiefs had little interest in what we

---

2 "Summary of District Three's 'Quick Win' Initiative: The Historic Concordia/Wells Street Neighborhood Policing Plan," internal report for MPD, 2008.

3 "Progress Report: Historic Concordia/Avenues West Neighborhood Policing Plan," internal report for MPD, February 19, 2008, p. 4.

were doing. We were now going to have an opportunity to show-case our district, as well as our officers and their talents directly to the chief, who would personally be attending the kickoff event. The cops were amazed at this. Part of the reason the cops were so accepting and did not heavily resist [Flynn as an outsider] is that he actually talked to them, and even got to know some of them by their first names in relatively short order. That was huge.[4]

An important outcome then for the MPD itself lay in seeing how the new chief would operate. Chief Flynn was clearly not a microman-ager, for he was intent upon identifying talented individuals at every level, and leveraging their abilities and creative instincts to work inde-pendently in pursuit of the new mission. In seeking contact and direct involvement at every level of the organization—attending roll calls as easily as command staff meetings—Chief Flynn offered his support for and investment in the ground-level work of police officers in the community as well as support for mid- and top-level administrators.

Improve Information Technology Operations

Flynn's third immediate effort was to develop a fully functioning information technology capacity. A major stumbling block for his plans for "community-based, problem-oriented, *data-driven*" (em-phasis added) policing was that the MPD's databases were a mess. Contemporary policing relies heavily on real-time data. Especially since the development of the compstat method in the New York City Police Department during the mid-1990s, police have learned that effective crime prevention requires intimate and timely familiarity with who is doing what to whom as well as where, when, and how to ensure appropriate intervention and assessment of those interven-tions. Neither data based planning nor assessments were possible in Milwaukee without an effective accurate system for data collection and analysis; as Chief Flynn recollected: "I couldn't generate reliable data on a daily basis."[5] Moreover, neither the MPD nor the city it-self seemed to have the capacity to solve the information technology problems. Not possessing the capacity to make the systems work was one difficulty; in addition, the MPD was unable to articulate its prob-lems to the system's vendor, or know if or when the vendor was simply obfuscating.

---

4   Deputy Chief James Harpole, MPD, undated memo to George Kelling.
5   Chief Edward Flynn, MPD, interview by George Kelling, June 27, 2011.

Lacking financial resources as well as capacity, Flynn turned to Milwaukee's corporate sector to see if he could get *pro bono* assistance. His opportunity came one week after he was appointed chief when he was invited to speak to the Greater Milwaukee Committee, a private sector civic organization committed to fostering Milwaukee's economic and cultural development. After explaining that timely accurate data were as important in policing as they were in any private sector business, Flynn laid out a request: "I need help making what I have work and I need help making the vendor give me what I deserve."[6] Two organizations immediately offered their expertise: Syslogic and Johnson Controls. Syslogic would make the MPD's system work and Johnson Controls would help deal with the vendor.[7]

The volunteer from Syslogic was its chairperson and chief executive officer, Tina Chang. Ms. Chang, a well-known young entrepreneur in the Milwaukee area, was not only a deeply respected businessperson but also the recipient of many civic awards for community service. From her point of view, five issues were of potential concern regarding the MPD's information technology systems: hardware, administrative leadership, software, selection methodology, and data. For the most part, hardware was not an issue: the MPD had appropriate hardware but just could not make it work properly. Perhaps the main problem from Ms. Chang's point of view was the fitness of IT leadership. The MPD had made the same mistake as many other organizations: it attempted to promote people from inside the organization who possessed other skills—such as being a good police administrator—but had relatively limited IT background to oversee its development and maintenance. For Ms. Chang this was a problem that created impossible expectations: IT administration required a set of competencies too complicated to be developed as a secondary interest by a police officer.[8] In other words, the IT system needed specialists in IT.

6   Chief Edward Flynn, MPD, interview by George Kelling, April 2, 2014.

7   It is ironic that Flynn turned to the Greater Milwaukee Committee for assistance. In 1990, GMC president Robert Milbourne went to MPD Chief Phillip Arreola to offer the group's help in improving the department's data system. Incredibly, Arreola turned Milbourne down. See "Can Chief Flynn Modernize the Police Department?," *Milwaukee MAG.Com*, January 22, 2008. Accessed November 24, 2014, http://www.MilwaukeeMag.com.

8   Ms. Chang was not the first departmental outsider to view the management of MPD IT efforts by police officers rather than IT professionals as

Linked to the administrative/leadership problem was the issue of the software. Most decisions regarding software selection had heretofore been made based on the "bells and whistles" of what vendors had to offer. A better approach would have been to select software based upon careful analysis of the MPD's needs. This required that the MPD have a clear and detailed vision of its mission—which, aside from responding to calls for service, it had lacked previously. The absence of technical leadership, a poor process for the selection of software, and a lack of vision had led previous administrations to purchase inadequate software. Furthermore, this inadequate software was not implemented to the best of its limited potential. The result was an operational system that produced "messy, dirty, unorganized data" largely useless in supporting Flynn's vision of a neighborhood data-based crime prevention strategy. Finally as Ms. Chang noted, the data that did exist were in silos: inventory had its database, detectives theirs, each special unit its own, and so on throughout the department. An audit discovered eighty-two discrete, unconnected data sets when Flynn took over the MPD.[9] Each unit had its own database and used the data to maintain its own autonomy. Flynn's vision was that IT would coordinate data across the entire organization.

Today these problems have been largely resolved. Ms. Chang serves on a Technical Advisory Committee that reviews the continued development and maintenance of the MPD's IT capabilities and an IT specialist is on the MPD's staff (a hard sell to city government). But even more importantly, data are readily available across unit boundaries, both informing a neighborhood strategy and operating against the continuation or development of silos; compstat is maintained and informed by the IT capacity; and data are used to provide officers with information both vital to their function of crime prevention and essential to their own safety in the conduct of their work. The old

---

a major source of data handling problems. A 1996 report by Milwaukee's comptroller found a $7.3 million IT project largely unsuccessful, blaming "the project's failures on the department's use of police officers rather than IT professionals to handle the project." Ibid.

9   Joel Plant (MPD Chief of Staff), interview by George Kelling, April 27, 2014.

software is not the best, but it is being used more effectively, to the utmost of its capability.[10]

The Calls for Service Dilemma

The fourth immediate issue Flynn confronted was how to assist district commanders in dealing with a dispatch system centered around 911 calls for service that still dominated Milwaukee policing. During the 1950s and 1960s American police established the goal of responding to all calls for service within three minutes, referred to in many departments as "full service policing." As crime continued to rise and neighborhood foot patrols declined, the demand via 911 quickly exceeded the capacity of virtually all police departments not just to respond in three minutes but on a timely basis at all. As calls queued and police ran from call to call, departments countered by prioritizing responses: calls where life or property was in danger got immediate attention; others that involved issues such as nuisances or business/customer disputes would get a delayed response. Such prioritization made sense, but it did not solve the problem of officers going from call to call, leaving them no time to engage in crime prevention.[11] Sending a car became the mode of police work—to do *what* was not always clear, but at least if a car was sent police believed they were doing their job.

To counter this axiom and provide neighborhood patrol officers with more time to work at crime prevention in their patrol areas, Flynn considered the feasibility of MPD responding to some calls via telephone, using fully trained sworn officers to cope with non-emergency calls. The issue was, as Flynn put it rhetorically: "What is it that actually requires the armed authority of the state in your living room right now? It's very expensive, and if we're not careful, all our officers are in houses giving advice and none of them are in the public space preventing crime!"[12] As an alternative, Chief Flynn reassigned a group

---

10   Tina Chang (Syslogic chair and chief executive officer), interview by George Kelling, April 25, 2014.

11   Not only that, many citizens in high crime areas, concerned about minor neighborhood problems and knowing about prioritization, learned how to defeat the system and get an immediate response regardless of the nature of the problem by reporting "man with a gun."

12   Chief Edward Flynn, personal conversation with George Kelling, March 14, 2008.

of 116 officers who had been on light-duty work due to illness or some other form of incapacitation: in district stations they answered phones, took reports, and conducted other forms of clerical work; and in headquarters they maintained the garage, kept it clean, handed out keys, and signed out cars—all tasks well below their training and skills. Creating the Differential Response Unit (DPU) in two districts (Two and Five) on an experimental basis in April of 2008, Flynn used these fully trained officers to provide police services in appropriate matters via telephone. The types of calls the DPU handled included civil matters such as business disputes, nuisance calls, loud noises, animal bites, parenting problems (where no violence or threat of violence was present), and other such concerns. Police counseled, referred, provided information and provided services in the same fashion they would have had they actually gone to the location of the call. If citizens insisted that a police officer should come to the scene or the DPU officer became aware of some threat of or actual violence, the matter would be returned to a dispatcher to send an available car. Pleased with the results Flynn went citywide in August of the same year. Since 2008, about 40,000 calls a year have been handled by the DPU. Follow up telephone surveys consistently find that three quarters of those citizens handled by DPU are either satisfied or very satisfied with police handling of their problem.[13]

These four early efforts—providing a vision, quick wins, developing competent information technology, and managing calls for service— were not the kind of innovations with which anyone found much to quarrel. Nor were they particularly hard to implement. They were important, however, in laying the groundwork for what was to come. Flynn's persistent focus on the MPD's community mission began to unite the MPD. Quick wins elaborated a sense of renewed mission and opened the doors to other agencies and neighborhoods and communities. Improved information technology created the capacity to identify and analyze problems on a real time basis. And the increased control over calls for service created additional patrol time that could be used to pursue the future core mission—developing and maintaining civic life. But Flynn's plans also included substantial changes to challenge the culture that had developed in MPD over the years, one in which a large number of officers and managers had vested interests: the cultural dominance of the Criminal Investigation Bureau and the

13 "DPR Overview," internal MPD memorandum, April 22, 2014.

elitism of special units. In Flynn's view, these were autonomous units continuing to pursue their own agendas.

REORGANIZING SPECIAL UNITS—THE CREATION OF THE NEIGHBORHOOD TASK FORCE

From the beginning a key concern of Chief Flynn was the functioning of the MPD's special units—intelligence, drug, street crime, and TAC (the Tactical Enforcement Unit). Such units pose opportunities and problems for police administrators. Clearly they can serve important purposes, especially in large departments like Milwaukee. Some problems cut across precinct/district lines, and require special skills and expertise by officers who address them. SWAT and TAC-like units may need relief from other duties because officers require constant practice to maintain their coordination, discipline, and skills. Some units are best centrally administered: for example, Internal Affairs to ensure that complaints against police are handled with appropriate accountability and according to a uniform procedure.

Notwithstanding such justifications, special units pose serious problems as well. First, whether intended or not, special units demean the work of patrol officers. "Important" police work—at least by the standards of the reform model of policing—is left to special units. Second, special units present accountability problems, especially at the precinct/district level. Community policing is built on the ideas that most crime problems are local; that solutions to these problems must be developed at a local level in cooperation with individuals, neighborhoods, and community institutions; that police should be organized around such community/neighborhood geographical areas; and that those "in charge" of such geographical areas (captains, commanders, inspectors—depending on the city) are accountable for both the quality of life and quality of policing in them. Centrally controlled special units dilute the ability of district commanders to achieve their goals and/or be held accountable. Discretion as to when and where special units are to be deployed resides almost solely with centralized decision making, not through the priorities identified in police districts. Such centralized decision-making may or may not benefit the city as a whole, but it is small comfort to the commander who, to use gangs as an issue, is struggling to manage violence on her/his own not knowing if, when, or where the gang unit is operating. Too often special units "cream" talent from districts—recruiting the best and brightest away from patrol—and develop their own agendas and priorities that may or may not be consistent with neighborhood priorities.[14]

Third, as line patrol officers often complain, officers in special units frequently lack knowledge of a local area and its players that is crucial to solving problems there. As an example, Milwaukee's early Tactical Enforcement Unit (known as TAC) was widely seen as an "occupying" force, especially by citizens in the African American community. TAC officers were quick to use pre-emptive force to handle situations and impose order. TAC officers were intended to appear fierce: their physical size and the number of officers per car (three), brandishing shotguns sent out a message that they would overwhelm any opposition. Even former members of the TAC squad during the 1980s and 1990s refer to the TAC officers during its earlier inception as the MPD's "big goons." This emphasis on pre-emptive threat or use of force, arguably used indiscriminately, is what bothered both citizens and the TAC squad's patrol colleagues. Patrol officers work regularly in neighborhoods and come to know both the troublemakers and the peacemakers (or those who at least will not interfere with or hassle police officers). When trouble breaks out, this familiarity helps them to manage situations as well as maintaining or restoring order. For instance: two neighbors have an argument; other neighbors begin to watch the dispute; family members get involved; some bystanders egg the disputants on, others try to settle things; soon fifty people are watching or involved in what is going on. What starts as an argument between two people morphs into a major neighborhood dispute by the time police are called and respond. Most neighborhood patrol officers know and can spot almost immediately who the disputants are, and probably know the origins of the dispute (the officers likely have been called to the location before) as well as who to approach and how.

Such neighborhood familiarity, however, is rare among special units. Most operate citywide and may be unfamiliar with specific neighborhoods, the residents, the history of problems, and who the

14 I knew this to be a problem for district commanders in Milwaukee even before Flynn became chief. In my early consultation, several commanders complained about the special units, especially the problem of "creaming" talent. It was not just that officers were pulled from patrol into special units, but often the best and most productive officers were pulled from patrol.

troublemakers and the peacemakers are. Their approach is not to persuade but to overwhelm the situation with, as police would put it, "kickin' ass and takin' names"—that is, the indiscriminate use of threat and force to solve problems and to manage conflicts. While this approach might quell the dispute for the moment, it does not address the ongoing problem; furthermore, it often generates resentment among the citizen peacemakers and passive observers who likely have been treated in the same fashion as the troublemakers.[15]

Fourth and finally, special units may be effective but can outlive their usefulness. Suppose that a special unit is created to deal with illegitimate gun carrying, especially by those with criminal histories. Suppose further that the officers are properly trained and conduct their activities legally, constitutionally, and well within the guidelines of the department. A primary metric for such units in many departments is the number of weapons they confiscate. And suppose that they are successful: as a result of the unit's activities, fewer people carry and use weapons illegitimately. If success is achieved in these terms, fewer guns will be confiscated over time (since fewer people are carrying weapons illegitimately). This puts such units in a quandary: the primary indicator of their success—confiscated guns—shows a decline. So what are the options? Widen the net (change the standards for stop, question, and frisk)? Reduce the size of the unit? Disband the unit? Change the function of the unit? What happens all too often

---

15   A senior commander describes this in Milwaukee: "[T]he regular patrol officers referred to the tactical officers as the 'golden boys.' The officers on the [tactical] unit got this name mainly because they were untouchable, would enter a scene and take action (arrest, use force, etc.) but would hand everything off to the district to handle and drive off in their all white, unmarked squads three officers deep. While the city was very busy and the district cars were running from assignment to assignment, the tactical cops had plenty of time to eat and just take it easy, picking and choosing the assignments they wanted to respond to. There was a chicken restaurant, Gold Rush Chicken, at Twenty-seventh and North that was the nightly eating spot for a good portion of the tactical unit officers. Detectives also spent a lot of time at the same restaurant. The district patrol cops referred to it as the tactical or CIB sub-station. Frequently, detectives would leave crime scenes, send the district officers downtown to start all of the paperwork, process evidence, and process arrested suspects while they first stopped and spent hour or so eating and chucking it up with tactical unit cops." Email communication with George Kelling, August 5, 2014.

in police departments is that these decisions are not made; rather, the unit goes on applying the same techniques (stop, question, and frisk) to deal with what might be a very different problem, such as disorderly behavior by juveniles.

What Flynn found in the MPD when he took office was two special divisions—Intelligence and Vice Control—that contained all the special units: Narcotics, Drug Interdiction, Prostitution, Gambling and Fugitive Apprehension, and the Gang Crimes Section. All were operating similarly and were centrally controlled. All set their own agendas (based largely informants' information), operated in plain clothes (Flynn referred to their Green Bay Packers tee shirts and jeans as "uniforms"), drove unmarked Ford Crown Victorias (which Flynn believed were as conspicuous to offenders as marked patrol cars), and concentrated on making drug arrests. While they did make a lot of arrests, Flynn believed they contributed little to the overall mission of the MPD: reducing crime, fear and disorder, and protecting the integrity of neighborhoods. Moreover, their operation was inconsistent with the goal of holding district commanders accountable for addressing problems in their respective geographical areas. Flynn believed that when district problems required additional skills or personnel, how and when they were to be used should properly be at the discretion of the district commander who ultimately had to answer for her/his district, not a centralized administrator.

Yet Flynn had to move cautiously. Special units were part of the MPD culture. They contained many talented officers with special skills. And at times they were needed. Maintaining a SWAT-like capacity to deal with extraordinary events like a shooter in a school was essential; so too, serving warrants to known violent offenders required special handling. Flynn's solution was to create the Neighborhood Task Force that was comprised of the Motorcycle, Canine, Tactical Enforcement, Street Crimes, Fugitive Apprehension, Marine, and Mounted Patrol Units, and ultimately headed by a captain.[16] The Marine and Mounted Patrol Units were later transferred to District One (the downtown/Lake Michigan area where those services are most often provided). The NTF was linked to each of the seven districts for operational purposes.

---

16   City of Milwaukee Memorandum 2008-67, May 29, 2008.

The deployment of NTF personnel will largely be dictated by the needs of the district commanders based upon tangible crime data and analysis. NTF deployments will be prioritized on efforts to 1) suppress violent crime, 2) restore and maintain order in neighborhoods, and 3) provide visible police presence in public spaces to reduce fear.

The NFT will work closely with district commanders in identifying targeted areas for deployment. Targeted areas will be identified by district commanders and intelligence obtained internally and from neighborhood sources.[17]

MPD's current "Operational Strategy" locates administrative functions of the NTF in the North Command Bureau; however, operationally special units contained in the NTF cooperate directly with district commanders based on neighborhood priorities.[18] Unless reasons exist to preclude it, officers in special units are uniformed and operate out of marked police vehicles. Units maintain their special functions through training and practice, and are available when their unique skills are required.[19] The following example documents the use of a special unit—the Tactical Enforcement Unit—in a multi-district, multi-unit, and multi-agency response to a serious crime problem. At the proper time, in coordination with the other units, and under the guidance of other units, the TEU is called in to ply its special skills.

During the early morning of March 29, 2014, shots were fired on Milwaukee's near north side (District Five). Investigators recovered

---

17   Ibid., p. 2.

18   See below in Chapter 6, pp. 25-26 including Figures 2 and 3, MPD Organizational Charts for October 2012 and September 2014, which illustrate the reorganization of the MPD from a functional to geographically based structure.

19   For example, part of the NTF—the Tactical Enforcement Unit—would maintain its current operations but also have new functions. "This unit shall be responsible for providing a proactive police presence in targeted areas aimed at driving down violent and street level crime and disorder through directed patrol." This emphasizes their NTF role. But the description goes on: "This component shall also be responsible for all medium and high-risk search warrants and incident management including, but not limited to, hostage, terrorist, barricaded persons, armed suicidal and hazardous surveillance." See "Re-organization, Modification to Departmental Divisions of Service," City of Milwaukee General Order No. 2008-20, May 29, 2008, p. 2.

seven 9mm casings at the scene. A casing from this incident was entered into the National Integrated Ballistics Information Network (NIBIN)—a ballistic imaging process and network that allows for comparison among casings. A day later, investigators recovered 9mm casings from a March 30 armed robbery of a pizza restaurant on the far north side of Milwaukee (District Seven). The casings from the two events matched. MPD Detective Robert Rehbein and Alcohol, Tobacco, Firearms, and Explosives (ATF) Special Federal Agent John Lindeman were assigned to the case. Based on rough images contained in a surveillance video of the first event provided by the Milwaukee Housing Authority, consultations with Detective John Ivy (North Investigations Division) who was working on a series of commercial robberies, and victims' descriptions of the robbers' *modus operandi* (MO) during the 30 March restaurant robbery, Rehbein and Lindeman worked with Officer John Amberg of the MPD Intelligence Fusion Center (IFC) to identify at least nine other similar commercial armed robberies that occurred between March 15 and April 23 on the northwest side of Milwaukee. Seven of these were robberies of auto parts stores and two of restaurants. The MO was similar: most robberies occurred within thirty minutes of closing time, the three perpetrators always demanded access to the safe, they often ordered employees to the rear of the business, most often they fled through a back door, and they expressed a willingness to use violence (one employee was shot). Rough descriptions of the three robbers indicated they were African American males between the ages of eighteen and twenty-five, two were over six feet tall, one was about five feet seven inches tall, all three wore white facemasks and displayed handguns.

On May 1, the District Three Captain convened representatives from Districts Three, Five, and Seven, North Investigative Division (NID), the Intelligence Fusion Center (IFC), and Alcohol, Tobacco, and Firearms (ATF) to share information. ATF offered a $5,000 reward for information leading to the arrest and conviction of the suspects. In addition, while reviewing MPD records, especially traffic stops, Fusion analysts discovered that three African American males had been stopped several times in the vicinity of robberies either immediately before or after they took place. Their descriptions roughly matched those of the robbery suspects. All had records of minor offenses. IFC staff searched Internet open sources and found numerous pictures of the suspects carrying firearms and wearing clothing similar to those worn during the commission of the crimes. Based on MPD records and the open sources data, police obtained a subpoena to search cellphone records. Analysis of these records placed the suspects in the vicinity of several of the robberies; however, data were not accurate enough to provide probable cause for arrest.

After a lull of about a month following the April 23 robbery, the robbers became active again, hitting two auto parts stores on May 28 and two more on June 1. On May 5, representatives of NID, ATF, IFC and Districts Two, Three, Four, Five, and Seven met to establish a directed patrol mission. A pole camera was installed overlooking the residences of one of the suspects. The districts would provide surveillance by patrol officers of likely targets. The IFC and ATF would conduct ongoing surveillance of the suspects ("tailing" them), both to gather intelligence and to identify pre-robbery activities. The Tactical Enforcement Unit (TEU) was alerted to be on an on-call status if pre-robbery activity was noted or a robbery occurred. Since this was primarily an intelligence gathering operation undercover personnel were ordered not to confront the suspects. Instead an attempt would be made by the TEU to stop the suspects if pre-robbery activities were identified and the TEU was in a position to do so. In the event that the TEU could not intervene immediately to stop the robbery, the suspects would not be confronted in the store but would be followed by surveillance units until they could be stopped by the TEU.

On June 6, surveillance units noted what they considered to be pre-robbery behavior: the suspects met, changed into clothing matching that described by victims, wore gloves, and changed cars. The TEU was alerted to respond to the area. Two of the suspects drove to a location near an auto parts store and parked. Shortly thereafter, two district officers on static surveillance at that location noted two masked men enter the auto supply store. Moments later the masked men exited, quickly went to their parked car, and left the scene. The active surveillance team followed them until the TEU arrived and activated their emergency lights to make a felony traffic stop. One of the suspects threw a gun out of his car window. The two suspects were taken into custody. They ultimately confessed to the robberies and identified the third suspect.[20]

---

20   Summary of narrative by Deputy Chief James Harpole, MPD, October 18, 2014.

This example, of course, demonstrates much more than the restrained use of the TEU. It is an example of internal collaboration and teamwork that is essential in a high performing organization. Captains exert leadership and initiative. Each unit carries out its responsibility as designed. Consequently risk is reduced for the robbery victims, the police, and the perpetrators. But just as special units have a new role in such an organization, detectives do as well.

REDEFINING THE ROLE OF DETECTIVES

As Flynn saw it when he took office, detectives in the MPD would be more effective if ways could be found to capitalize on their skills and put them to service in achieving the core mission of the department—crime prevention. The rationale undergirding Flynn's subsequent moves was that during the conduct of inquiries into particular cases, such as homicides, investigators obtained information about contextual problems that might be relevant to other cases or even give rise to other crimes. An example would be the murder of a gang member. It is not unlikely that if one gang member kills or shoots at a member of another gang, this action will set off a cycle of revenge shootings and homicides. An investigation carried out by detectives can provide information that if properly handled and communicated may become useful intelligence for patrol officers, detectives, and special units attempting to stop the next shooting or homicide. This means that detectives have a broader responsibility than investigating cases and preparing them for prosecution: their special skills in gathering information, if properly exploited, can enhance a police department's crime prevention capacity. Unfortunately this potential has rarely been realized in American policing and certainly was not the case in the MPD where the CIB had successfully insulated itself from all other units

Flynn's initial move was to involve detectives in daily morning crime briefings for the command staff, a first in the history of the MPD. He then assigned a career detective to head the patrol division and a career patrol commander to head the CIB (Criminal Investigation Bureau). While there was nothing new in assigning a detective to head patrol, the assignment of a patrol commander to head CIB was unheard of. No longer would patrol be subordinate to CIB. Management systems were put in place in the MPD, as noted in a Harvard/National Institute of Justice publication, "to address a bureau that was rife with antiquated processes and procedures, lacked technology systems, paid little attention to performance measures, and lacked quality financial oversight."[21] New emphasis was placed on property crime so that detectives, rather than operating citywide on particular types of property crimes, were assigned to investigate all types within particular neighborhoods. Most detectives were placed under the command of decentralized geographic bureaus (North, South, Central), with only homicide, drugs, sex, and computer crime investigations functioning from "downtown"—homicide because it is so specialized, and drugs, sex, and computer crimes because they cross district and city lines.

In 2013 Flynn undertook a more comprehensive reorganization within the MPD as a whole, replacing its traditional functional type of organization (comprised of Patrol, Investigation, and Administration Bureaus) with a geographically based organization made up of South, Central, and North Commands. Each of these included an Investigation Division headed by an assistant chief. Specialized investigations (narcotics and homicide) remained centralized. Figures 2 (MPD Organizational Chart, October 2012) and 3 (MPD Organizational Chart, September 2014) that follow illustrate the change in MPD from a functionally to a geographically based organization. [See Figures 2 and 3 that follow on separate pages].

---

21   Braga et al., "Moving the Work of Criminal Investigators Towards Crime Control," 16.

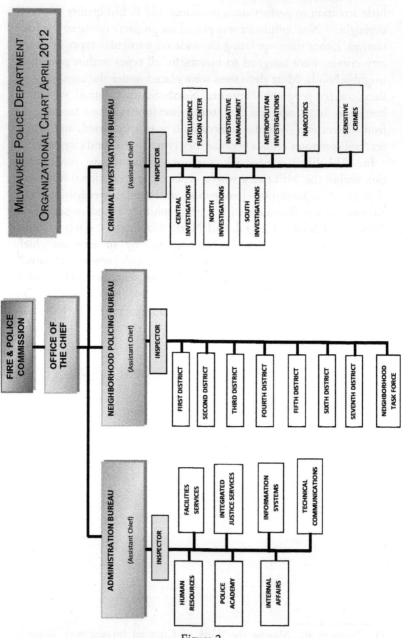

Figure 2
Milwaukee Police Department Organizational Chart October 2012
(Source: Milwaukee Police Department, November 29, 2014)

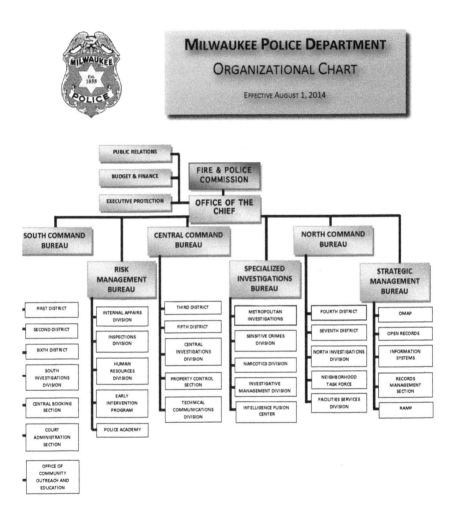

Figure 3
Milwaukee Police Department Organizational Chart
Effective September 23, 2014
(Source: Milwaukee Police Department, November 29, 2014)

As stated in a 2014 MPD memorandum:

> The purpose of the reorganization was to shift the work of the
> CIB from a reactive detective unit engaged primarily in retrospec-
> tive investigations and clearance rates as a measure of success, to
> one that is proactive and focused on crime prevention and reduc-
> tion, through a collaborative working relationship with our district
> partners, while focusing our finite resources on geography and the
> neighborhoods that make up that geography. ...
>
> It is our goal to be on the cutting edge of a national movement
> to innovate detective units and move their work towards crime
> prevention in the community-policing context. In order to do so,
> changes in the investigative structure to better align our resources
> toward a data-driven, intelligence-led, problem-solving, and neigh-
> borhood-focused strategies are necessary.[22]

The case that follows is a recent example of detectives being involved
in a team operation with other units of the MPD. Their roles are pre-
ventative as well as investigative. Patrol officers and data analysts are
their colleagues.

In June of 2014, crime analysts from the MPD's Intelligence Fusion
Center and detectives based geographically in districts noted almost
simultaneous increases in armed robbery and auto theft across the
city.[23] The timing and locations of crime incidents suggested that increases in the two might be related. On the night of June 23rd, a fif-
teen-year-old boy who was attempting an armed robbery was shot and
seriously wounded by his intended victim. Four nights later thirteen
other juveniles, who ran out of gas in the two cars they had stolen,
hijacked a car in a residential neighborhood. Spotted by police, the
youths led them on a high-speed chase, finally running over deployed
spike strips. Eleven of the thirteen juveniles were then apprehended.
Interrogations by Detectives Shawn Halverson (working out of South

---

22   Internal Memorandum, Milwaukee Police Department, February 28,
     2014, pp. 1-2.

23   Fusion centers in police departments grew out of the 9/11 terrorist at-
     tacks, specifically the need to gather, analyze, and share data and intelli-
     gence about terrorism among and within police agencies. As fusion centers
     matured it became clear that such centers could conduct crime analysis
     as well. Currently, in most cities crime analysis is their primary function.
     Regarding detectives, with the few exceptions noted above they have shift-
     ed to operating geographically out of the three Divisions: North (Districts
     Four and Seven), South (One, Two, and Six) and Central (Three and Five).

District Two) and John Ivy (working out of North District Seven) revealed that at least two of the youths had been present on June 23rd when their companion was shot.

Despite these apprehensions and the information gathered, car thefts and armed robberies continued as the summer progressed. Trying to understand in depth what was going on, Halverson and Ivy, working with crime analyst Officer Eric Draeger (from the Fusion Center), conducted network analyses. They used information gathered from in-custody suspects, existing intelligence about Milwaukee's crews obtained from monitoring of crews' communications and other sources, data available on social media, and the knowledge of patrol officers in all seven districts who were familiar both with crews and crew members in their districts. Putting all of this together, police could see that crews were operating citywide.

As the Fusion Center continued its analyses, patterns emerged: crews that were originally thought to be separate were often connected through one or two people in each group. Multiple cars were stolen, some set aside for future use, in carrying out the armed robberies. Robberies were conducted by several carloads of youths for the specific purpose of making it difficult for witnesses or victims to identify the perpetrator(s). Stolen cars used in robberies were abandoned after a robbery, and the youths changed clothing after each offense. All were signs of a carefully planned set of offenses.

Putting this all together—the timing, location, intelligence, and patterns—the Fusion Center was able identify the crews and individuals that were likely involved and provide this information to an ad hoc robbery task force that had been created under the command of Captain Eric Moore and Lieutenant William Beauchene, and to the affected districts. Shortly after one large crew was identified, an intended victim shot and killed one of its members: all but two of the suspects were arrested within twenty-four hours. The remaining suspects were also soon in custody. To apprehend one, detectives worked closely with district officers who set up surveillance in several places he was known to hang out. Patrol officers in the Seventh District took him into custody a few days later. Detective Ivy then reached out to Seventh District Police Officer Melissa Takacs, who established rapport with the family of the suspect remaining at large. Officer Takas was able to arrange for this last suspect to turn himself in to police without incident.

Despite this success, armed robberies continued at high levels. At least one crew that had been arrested was out of jail and again committing robberies, using the same operating pattern. Ultimately an officer observed a vehicle that had been stolen at gunpoint, pursued it, and with colleagues arrested all five of these crew members. Through continued monitoring, especially of social media, detectives and analysts were able to track suspects they believed to be involved in other incidents. Within a month police took eight different crews into custody. In the end, thirty-six suspects were charged with 189 counts of robbery and auto theft.[24]

In all, this operation was a major effort by the MPD requiring coordination among division detectives, district patrol officers and their commanders in all seven districts, a citywide ad hoc task force, and staff from the centralized fusion center. As Captain Moore put it: "This was all in real time. The crews were very busy. At times we were knocking on their doors as they were committing robberies. But working together we finally closed them down."

SPECIAL ISSUES: TRAFFIC ENFORCEMENT AND THE JOURNAL SENTINEL

In the first months of his tenure, Flynn dealt with a number of other issues: bringing overtime under control (a sore point at city hall); providing leadership training for every member of the department; involving the private sector as a partner with the MPD whenever possible; and "branding" the organization in a way that reflected its new mission. In terms of specific crime problems, Flynn believed that aggressive traffic enforcement had potential as a means to prevent crime and adjusted the MPD's tactics accordingly. At the same time, as a major impediment to his work Milwaukee's sole major newspaper, the *Journal Sentinel*, declared "war" on Chief Flynn.

Traffic Enforcement

In the summer of 2008, primarily influenced by a 1978 article by James Q. Wilson and Barbara Boland, Chief Flynn initiated a traffic enforcement program to aid in crime control. The Wilson/Boland article examined the relationship between traffic enforcement and

---

24   Summary of narrative by Deputy Chief James Harpole, MPD, October 18, 2014.

robbery, concluding that aggressive enforcement against moving violations deterred street robbery.[25] Wilson and Boland's explanation for the deterrent effect of traffic enforcement was that "by stopping, questioning, and otherwise closely observing citizens, especially suspicious ones, the police are more likely to find fugitives, detect contraband (such as stolen property or concealed weapons), and apprehend persons fleeing from the scene of a crime."[26] At the time, the article caught relatively little attention and had little impact on policing. It was outside the box of police thinking.

In respects this finding was consistent with broken windows theory: enforcement of laws against minor offenses, including traffic infractions, gives police a broad base of contact with citizens. Most of these individuals are law-abiding and only need reminders to behave; nevertheless a substantial number are chronic offenders, including serious offenders. This was the experience in the New York City subway where it was discovered that a high percentage of those who did not pay their fares were either carrying illegal weapons or wanted on a felony warrant; in other words, not all fare beaters were found to be criminals but many criminals were fare beaters. Likewise, there is good reason to believe that not all traffic offenders are criminals but many criminals are traffic offenders. Data collected by the MPD as of 2014 confirm that a small number of bad drivers not only were committing a high percentage of traffic offenses, but other criminal offenses as well. These data show specifically:

+ Twelve of the fourteen most prolific offenders had been arrested a total of ninety-four times by the MPD on 245 charges.

+ Seven of the fourteen were arrested at least thirty times for at least forty-five felonies.

+ These charges included: operating a vehicle without consent, probation violation, felony bail jumping, possession with intent to deliver marijuana, robbery, possession with intent to deliver

---

25   James Q. Wilson and Barbara Boland, "The Effect of Police on Crime," *Law and Society Review* 12, no. 3 (Spring 1978): 367-390.

26   Ibid., 373-374.

cocaine, burglary, felon in possession of a firearm, and motor vehicle theft.

• The most prolific traffic offender of 2013 had twenty-three arrests for seventy-eight charges including possession of marijuana, burglary, robbery and other minor and serious offenses.[27]

The problem with using traffic enforcement as a means of crime control, especially if one targets traffic enforcement at crime hotspots, is that it "taxes" (to use Flynn's term) the poor and minorities living in high crime areas. These individuals often drive older cars that present maintenance problems, and because police are more attentive to traffic in such areas, their driving will come under closer scrutiny than residents of low crime areas. Consequently, Flynn emphasized aggressive traffic enforcement but also implemented a policy of limited ticketing and extensive use of warnings. He addressed the danger of "over taxing" poor communities by closely monitoring traffic stops and citations in compstat, comparing how each officer stood in comparison with her/his peers working in the same district during the same shift. Outliers—those with an extraordinarily high or low number of traffic stops and/or citations—were noted, without assuming officer malfeasance or zealotry. Flynn is satisfied if sergeants can explain the reasons why an officer has unusually high or low numbers, and if corrective action is required, that sergeants are taking it. This is the process by which Flynn attempts to ensure that guidelines are followed, officers are held accountable for their activities, and there are no "quotas," that is a fixed number of car stops, warnings, and citations.

Figure 4 (next page) shows the increase in car stops, and the percent warned and cited during Flynn's administration.

---

27   Data provided by the MPD Office of Management, Analysis & Planning, May 1, 2014.

Figure 4
MPD Traffic Stop Outcomes, 2007-2013[28]

Year	Total Stops	Warned	Percent Warned	Cited	Percent Cited
2007	52,410	16,938	32%	35,472	68%
2008	62,042	24,980	40%	37,062	60%
2009	138,980	79,764	57%	59,216	43%
2010	191,055	126,657	66%	64,398	34%
2011	188,729	128,363	68%	60,366	32%
2012	196,913	144,095	73%	52,818	27%
2013	183,538	142,079	77%	41,459	23%

It is important to note that as traffic stops increased so too did the percentage of those warned rather than ticketed, increasing from 32 percent to 77 percent warned. In fact, while total traffic stops increased 250 percent from 2007 to 2013, the number of tickets given increased only 17 percent. During this time complaints against police dropped from 488 in 2007 to 206 in 2013, a decline of 59 percent.

While it is not possible to parse out the impact of traffic enforcement on crime prevention, it is important to note that the overlap between bad driving and crime is becoming a matter of national concern. The Departments of Justice and Transportation and the National Highway Traffic Safety Administration, for example, have developed a national program that they have called "Data-Drive Approaches to Crime and Traffic Safety" (DDACTS).[29] The MPD has been one of the lead agencies. Yet, as noted below, not all of the MPD's recent successes have been met with approval. Elements of Milwaukee's media have been highly critical of the MPD, targeting especially on Flynn.

The Media Controversy

For the most part, Flynn has had a relatively easy time leading the MPD. He has had strong support from Mayor Tom Barrett, the Fire and Police Commission, and the Common Council. Although the

---

28   Ibid.

29   See for example, *Data-Driven Approaches to Crime and Traffic Safety: Operational Guidelines*, U. S. Department of Justice, August, 2009.

Milwaukee Police Association resisted some of his innovations, especially the reorganization of the CIB, they have not been extraordinarily hostile. Line police respect him. And judging by his reception when in neighborhoods, he enjoys widespread popularity in the community. In my contacts with friends and interviews with community leaders and elites, I constantly hear things like "Flynn was exactly what Milwaukee needed," "the best chief we've ever had," "a great chief," and "the best Milwaukee police chief in modern memory." Yet for a good share of his tenure as police chief, he has struggled with Milwaukee's sole newspaper, the *Milwaukee Journal Sentinel.*

Until 1995 Milwaukee was a two-newspaper city: the *Sentinel* was a morning and the *Journal* an evening paper, although the *Journal* owned the *Sentinel* since the 1960s, having purchased it from the Hearst Corporation. Generally, the *Sentinel* was conservative and the *Journal* liberal, and this pattern was maintained even after the *Journal* purchased the *Sentinel.* In 1995 the two newspapers merged and became the *Journal Sentinel,* a morning paper.

While the struggle between public officials and the media is nothing new and goes with the territory, the antagonism of the *Journal Sentinel* toward Flynn was remarkable. In three series of articles spread over a thirteen-month period (August 2011-September 2012), the *Journal Sentinel* attacked Flynn's overall strategy, competence, and veracity at a time when Milwaukee was experiencing an unprecedented drop in crime. Each series was initiated with a "watchdog" story, and followed by subsequent articles headed by new leads but in substance reiterating the first story—thereby keeping the original charges in front of readers over many months.

The first series concerned a modest increase in response time to calls for service, making its argument by presenting anecdotes from disgruntled citizens whose calls had apparently been mishandled. On August 6, 2011, *Journal Sentinel* Watchdog Reporter Ben Poston published a major story: "Police response times lag as patrol strategy shifts ."[30] On October 18, 2011, Poston and the *Journal Sentinel* published a front-page story basically repeating the material from the original

---

30   Ben Poston, "Police Response Times Lag as Patrol Strategy Shifts," *Milwaukee Journal Sentinel,* August 6, 2011. http://www.jsonline.com/watchdogreports/127077973.html. The term "watchdog" is how the *Journal Sentinel* describes investigative journalism and investigative journalists.

story: "New records show slower police response time in Milwaukee."[31] The stories challenged Flynn's use of a crime prevention strategy as opposed to the mid-1950s strategy of responding to crime after the fact. Absent from the accounts were well-known research findings that Flynn had provided reporters regarding the questionable efficacy of responding rapidly to calls for service and arguments illustrating the potential of a crime prevention strategy.

The second series, by Watchdog Reporter Gina Barton, identified ninety-three officers on the force who had committed a variety of offenses during their careers and whose punishments did not appear sufficient to fit their offenses. On October 23, 2011, the *Journal Sentinel* published Barton's article "At least 93 Milwaukee police officers have been disciplined for violating law," the first of a three-part series that included photos of all 93 officers. [32] Barton omitted the fact that the cases had occurred over thirty-one years, with 86 percent taking place prior to Flynn's administration, and that median disciplinary suspensions for domestic violence and drunken driving increased from two days prior to Flynn's administration to thirty days during Flynn's tenure.

The third series, again by Watchdog Reporter Ben Poston, accused the MPD of purposely misreporting crime statistics in order to make it appear that serious crime had declined more than it actually had. On May 22, 2012, Poston began the report: "Hundreds of assault cases misreported by Milwaukee Police Department: City's violent crime rate lowered based on faulty data."[33] As commentators ranging from Common Council members and state politicians to academics

---

31   Ben Poston, "New Records Show Slower Police Response Time in Milwaukee," *Milwaukee Journal Sentinel*, October 18, 2011. http://www.jsnoline.com/news/milwaukee/shots-ring-out-why-bother-calling-police-132115243.html.

32   Gina Barton, "At Least 93 Milwaukee Police Officers Have Been Disciplined for Violating Law," *Milwaukee Journal Sentinel*, October 23, 2011. http://www.jsonline.com/watchdog/watchdogreports/at-least-93-officers-have-been-disciplined-for-violating-law-132268408.html.

33   Ben Poston, "Crimes Underreported by Police Include Robbery, Rape," *Milwaukee Journal Sentinel*, May 22, 2012. http://www.jsonline.com/watchdogreports/crimes-underreported-by-police-include-robbery-rape-e567cu0-167448105.html.

weighed in, Flynn ordered an internal audit.[34] The findings refuted all charges over the previous six years: aggravated assaults had decreased, classification errors were made in both directions—over-reporting and underreporting—and classification errors in the reporting of aggravated assault had decreased.[35]

In addition to the MPD's internal audit, the Fire and Police Commission contracted with PRI Management Group, a firm specializing in crime statistics audits, to conduct an audit of the MPD's crime statistics. Their findings were published in December 2012, and showed: first, the internal audit was reliable and valid; second, problems in the IT system, a lack of internal controls, deficient training, and individual performance had together led to the errors; and third, no efforts had been undertaken by the Milwaukee Police Department to intentionally alter or manipulate crime statistics.[36] The PRI Management Group report praised the MPD, and criticized Poston and the *Journal Sentinel*: "...the Department has a culture that embraces and promotes professionalism, integrity and accountability through management processes designed to measure performance of individual employees and the organization as a whole."[37] As for the *Journal Sentinel*, PRI rejected its stories point-by-point, article-by-article, noting the failure by reporters to include pertinent information, their use of flawed comparisons, and their inappropriate suggestions of "nefarious activity" by Flynn and the MPD.[38]

Things quieted down after the PRI report was released. Ben Posten left the *Journal Sentinel* before the PRI report was published to become assistant data editor at the *Los Angeles Times* (where currently he is

---

34 Two criminologists, neither of whom had any familiarity with Milwaukee or the MPD, got into the act: Ohio State University Professor Michael Maltz saying "Misreporting is cheating the public ... [the findings are] the tip of the iceberg" and University of Nebraska Omaha Professor Samuel Walker asserting "That [misreporting] clearly indicates a systemic problem in the department ... there has to be a failure of leadership."

35 "Chief Flynn Announces Initial Crime Data Results," press release, City of Milwaukee Police Department, June 21, 2012.

36 "Independent Audit of Milwaukee Police Crime Statistics and Reporting Procedure," unpublished report, PRI Management Group," December 2012, pp. 15-16.

37 Ibid.,15.

38 Ibid., 25-26.

writing about "faulty data" in the Los Angeles Police Department). Barton won the John Jay College/Harry Frank Guggenheim 2012 Excellence in Criminal Justice Reporting Award for her writing on the MPD; those giving the award took her story at face value, never checking its validity fully. Yet the impact of this "watchdog journalism" on the community, the MPD, and the chief is troubling. In each case, the reporters did identify problems: some calls for service were mishandled; some officers were not held accountable for illegal behavior; and mistakes were made in recording crimes. But when journalists had the opportunity to assess the department's *current response* to the problems they identified, they chose not to do so. For the MPD, the constant stream of articles constituted a distraction that required the department to defend itself from unwarranted attacks. The articles also reflected a failure by the media to recognize the complexity of strategic moves the MPD was making to reorganize itself and implement a genuine community policing strategy. No doubt the media gave plenty of ammunition to internal opponents of the strategic shifts underway in the MPD.

The distortion by the *Journal Sentinel* in its reporting were sufficiently obvious and exaggerated that throughout the series, Mayor Barrett, the majority of Milwaukee's Common Council, the Fire and Police Commission, former *Journal Sentinel* reporter Bruce Murphy (writing for *Milwaukee Magazine*), and other commentators fully supported the MPD and Chief Flynn. Charlie Sykes, a popular conservative talk show host and journalist wrote after the publication of the PRI report: "The report also delivers a stinging blow to the journalistic jihad waged against the chief by the Milwaukee Journal Sentinel, which has devoted thousands of words and slain whole forests in their attempt to suggest that Flynn has been fudging the numbers."[39] Even with such support, however, inaccurate and irresponsible reporting can cause a lot of damage, especially in a single newspaper city. For the community the primary casualty was trust. Could neighborhoods and communities that have had difficulties with the MPD in the past have confidence in the present that the department was moving ahead with a strategy that truly included all the elements of the community,

---

39 Charlie Sykes, "The Exoneration of Ed Flynn," WTMJ Blog, January 4, 2013. Accessed November 24, 2014, http://www.620wtmj.com/blogs/charliesykes/185611021.html.

that would hold MPD members accountable, and that would prevent crime?

As discouraging as the *Journal Sentinel* response to Flynn and the MPD was, substantial progress was being made in virtually all of Flynn's moves to develop data based, preventive, community policing.[40] District captains were exerting leadership and creating initiatives, detectives were moving out of their isolation, special units were accepting their new roles, and new partners were being developed to work with the MPD. The final, remaining task here is to assess the impact of MPD's evolution on the City of Milwaukee, and to determine whether the quality of life has improved for its citizens and neighborhoods.

---

40   Chief Flynn had also moved aggressively in two areas that the *Journal Sentinel* had championed over the years: out of control overtime and the failure of the IT systems. In each case, Flynn made substantial progress. Overtime was kept within budget; the private sector was assisting the MPD do the best it could with its existent computer system.

CHAPTER SEVEN

ASSESSING THE MILWAUKEE POLICE DEPARTMENT'S ACHIEVEMENTS UNDER CHIEF FLYNN

Through his vision of "community-based, problem-oriented, data-driven" policing, and the structural and administrative changes he has implemented, Chief Flynn has repositioned the MPD nationally where it now sits among the leading departments of community policing. These changes have included decentralizing authority (especially to district commanders), moving from a functionally to a geographically-based organization, empowering line officers to identify and solve problems within their work areas, integrating special units with patrol, and shifting detective work to include crime prevention as well as *post hoc* investigations of already committed crimes. In this final chapter we will examine some outcomes of the structural and procedural changes that Chief Flynn has undertaken, and of the specific crime control efforts he has pursued to date. We also look at what the MPD's recent achievements can tell us about community policing today.

CRIME REDUCTION AND OTHER INDICATORS OF ACHIEVEMENT

From 2007, the year before Flynn was appointed chief, to 2013, violent crime in Milwaukee declined 11 percent and property crime 31 percent; overall crime declined 27 percent. The extent to which these reductions in crime can be attributed to Chief Flynn's innovations is subject to debate. An extensive literature has developed about the reasons for the overall crime declines in the United States that have taken place in recent years. In many respects this debate may never be completely resolved—nor will we know why crime rose so dramatically during the second half of the twentieth century. Many factors have the potential to cause crime or allow it to flourish: family breakdown, poor education, drug marketing and use, child abuse, poverty, the erosion of traditional values that held particular behaviors in check, unemployment, and poor policing to name but a few. Likewise many factors can work to reduce crime: social programs, quality education, mentoring, employment, neighborhood and community crime control efforts, thoughtful and targeted policing, and business improvement districts (BIDS) are among them. But it is hard—especially given the experiences in cities like New York, Los Angeles, and now Milwaukee—to argue that smart policing does not play a major role in preventing crime and creating community security.[1] This does not mean that other community efforts are unimportant; nevertheless, they are inherently limited when offenders really get persistent. Only police possess the "or else" of force to enhance efforts at preventing crime and creating livable communities.

We should also recognize that crime statistics alone do not reflect the quality of policing in a community—the police role is complex and multifaceted. Clearly complaints against police tell us something about how police are performing, and in Milwaukee from 2007 to 2013, complaints dropped 59 percent (from 488 to 201). Calls for service also declined by 24 percent (from 317,584 to 241,423). Police use of force declined fifty percent (966 to 479). Police squadcar accidents declined thirty-three percent (252 to 169). Traffic stops increased by 254 percent; however, citations remained relatively constant (while stops rose from 52,410 to 185,358, citations from 35,472 to 41,459).[2] Police overtime was brought under control and kept within budget. Clearly it would be desirable to have additional data, especially concerning citizen perceptions about the quality of policing and their levels of fear of crime, but such data are not available. And admittedly many of the indicators identified above are surrogate measures of

1   See for example, Franklin E. Zimring, *The City that Became Safe: New York's Lessons for Urban Crime and Its Control* (New York: Oxford University Press, 2012).

2   Data were provided by the MPD's Office of Management and Planning, November 2014.

police achievements and productivity. Yet the fact that they all point in the desired direction adds weight to their credibility.

COMMUNITY POLICING:
REALITY OR "SMOKE AND WHISTLES"

Regardless of the strength of the indicators noted above, it is fair to ask at least two other questions which my experience gives me some grounds for answering. First, how close has the Milwaukee Police Department moved towards community policing, that is, given what we know about community policing how close does the MPD's current strategy "fit" a community-policing model? In a sense, I am asking whether Flynn's organizational and administrative changes are real or if the changes mask a "business as usual," centralized organization? Second, has the MPD restored itself as a leader in police thinking and development nationally? I begin with an example.

On May 10, 2010, Chief Edward Flynn appointed Captain Steven Basting and Lieutenant Karen Dubis to head District One, comprised of Milwaukee's downtown and an eastern swath along Lake Michigan that included the University of Wisconsin-Milwaukee campus, bordering on the City of Shorewood. Captain Basting had overall responsibility for the district with Lieutenant Dubis in charge of the night shift. Within days of these appointments, an attorney representing the American Civil Liberties Union (ACLU) confronted Basting and indicated that he was opposed to the MPD's handling of the homeless, especially in the downtown area, and would soon begin legal action against the city and the MPD.[3] But it was not just the ACLU that was

---

3   Captain Steven Basting, MPD, interview by George Kelling, January 7, 2014. I have been involved in developing police policies and practices in dealing with what has been called the "homeless" problem in at least three departments: New York Transit Police during the late 1980s and early 1990s, and the Los Angeles and Boston Police Departments during the early 2000s. The term homeless does little to illuminate what is in reality a complex set of problems. Those commonly referred to as homeless are comprised of at least four troubled/troublesome populations: the economic homeless, driven to the street by economic problems and the failure of social networks to keep them off the street; the mentally ill, most of whom are either unable to obtain services or refusing services; substance abusers, like the mentally ill either unable to obtain services or refusing them; and predators who mix in with the first three, often deal drugs and/or attack both the other three populations and the general population.

dissatisfied with the MPD's handling of the homeless; Chief Flynn was as well. In fact this was part of the reason he had assigned Basting and Dubis to District One.

The MPD's practices in dealing with the homeless at that time, not unusual in many cities, were to order them to "move on" or to ticket them for some kind of disorderly conduct. To be sure, some officers would attempt to persuade street dwellers to go to shelters and were reluctant to give tickets, but the decision about how to get people to move on or whether or not give a ticket was largely left to the unguided discretion of individual police officers. From a particular police point of view, however, the practice of writing a ticket even when officers knew that there was no possibility of the ticket being paid (and some homeless received hundreds of tickets), had value. When a major convention took place in town and city government wanted the downtown area to look spiffy, police conducted "warrant sweeps," using the accumulated arrest warrants that resulted from not paying the fines to jail homeless citizens during the convention. When the convention was over, those arrested were released and the whole process would be repeated: citation, citation not paid, warrant issued, convention, warrant sweep, arrest and jailing—a procedure as Lieutenant Dubis puts it "that degraded both police and the homeless."[4]

Beyond degrading everyone involved and its dubious legal and moral underpinnings, the MPD's handling of street people did not work. It did not help the street people; it did not help the downtown; and it did not improve the standing of the MPD in the community or with governmental and other agencies. Yet doing *something* about the homeless was important to Milwaukee's downtown. A 2005 survey conducted for Business Improvement District #21 (covering the downtown area) concluded: "Although crime is low in downtown Milwaukee, the perception of unsafe conditions at night also prevails.... Some describe the area as clean, filled with fine architecture

---

Acknowledging that there is considerable overlap among these populations does not change the reality that each requires a different approach by police or other agencies.

4   Lieutenant Karen Dubis, MPD, interview by George Kelling, January 9, 2014.

and friendly people. Others describe the area as smelly, run-down and filled with vagrants."[5]

In response Lieutenant Dubis began to look for alternatives to the MPD's approach. Noting that sessions at a Problem-Oriented Policing Conference in Arlington, Texas, were going to deal with managing the problem of street people, she requested permission to attend. There she familiarized herself with the award-winning HOT (Homeless Outreach Team) program in Colorado Springs, Colorado, the goals of which were to identify street people who presented chronic problems (so-called "frequent fliers" who consumed an enormous volume of police, EMT, and medical time at great cost but with little result),[6] and work with other agencies to ensure that proper services were provided to this population—one that was both at risk and threatened the viability of Colorado Springs's downtown.

Dubis returned to Milwaukee convinced that a program such as HOT could work there and she began to meet with agencies providing homeless services. She readily identified two highly competent, respected officers, and provided them with special training that focused on meeting the homeless in order to learn what their problems were, establishing a relationship with them, and referring them to appropriate sources of help. To the surprise of police their subsequent activities were met with open arms by the service agencies. Shelters that had previously closed their doors to additional clients at six p.m. allowed police to bring them in after closing. A priest who had written a letter to the police forbidding them to enter parish property because of their aggressive practices now willingly met with Basting and Dubis to tear up the letter, and encouraged police to visit as often as they liked. Agencies and parishes providing homeless services began regularly calling for police help, especially in dealing with predators who mixed in with the street population and victimized both them and other citizens. Special training was expanded to six officers and plans

---

5   http://www.milwaukeedowntown.com/images/content/downloads/2005BrandStatus_whitepaper.pdf

6   See, Malcolm Gladwell, "Million Dollar Murray," *New Yorker*, February 13, 2006, http://gladwell.com/million-dollar-murray/, for an example. Milwaukee had a similar case: a man who averaged eight "man down" calls a week in which police and EMTs responded and transported the person to an emergency room only to see him sobered up, released, and then proceed to drink himself again into unconsciousness.

were made to expand the entire program citywide, training all officers. Such training involves participation by community and agency
representatives as well as site visits by police trainees to shelters and
other agencies. New written policies regarding the MPD's handling of
street people were developed by Lieutenant Dubis and Officers James
Knapinski and Anthony Leino, the first two receiving special training.

To top off the effort, Lieutenant Dubis and the two officers received Milwaukee's prestigious 2011 Hope Award from Community
Advocates for their work with the homeless. Upon bestowing the
award Community Advocates Chief Executive Officer Joe Volk explained: "These officers know many of Milwaukee's chronically homeless people by name. Because of their work, families have been reunit-
ed, and men and women who just a few months ago had little chance
of a future are now moving toward independent living, and being safe
and secure in their own homes."[7] For Elizabeth Weirick, who heads
Milwaukee's Business Improvement District #21, the team of Basting
and Dubis has "contributed enormously to the changed culture of
Milwaukee's downtown, especially the nighttime economy. Police not
only got to know the homeless and their problems, they also got to
know business people, especially in entertainment, working with them
to control the problems associated with a nighttime as well as daytime
economy."[8]

This, in my mind, is an example of excellence in community policing—perhaps one that goes beyond common practice in the MPD but
nonetheless an illustration of what can be accomplished in the MPD
given its decentralization of authority, the willingness to learn from
its own shortcomings and from other police departments as well as
from the police literature, its development of working relationships
with other agencies, and the capitalization of talent at all levels of the
organization. In what follows I parse out elements from this example
that reflect a basic shift in policing paradigm for the MPD.

The first element to note is that the MPD recognized a chronic
problem (people living on the street) and that police handling of this
problem raised issues of civil rights, alienated police from the social

---

7   "Media Advisory," unpublished document, Community Advocates, May
    12, 2011. Community Advocates is a local service and advocacy organiza-
    tion in Milwaukee. See http://www.communityadvocates.net.

8   Elizabeth Weirick, personal interview by George Kelling, January 21,
    2014.

service community, and failed to contribute to the culture and economy of the redeveloping downtown area. The previous approach used citation, arrest, and jailing as a means of "sweeping" the streets, especially during periods when the city wanted the downtown to look good (such as during conventions or festivals). The need now was to better understand the problem, and find more acceptable and effective ways of dealing with it.

Second, a district captain and lieutenant were empowered to seek new ways to deal with this problem. Rather than assume that the problem would be best understood and planned for by central administration as had been traditional, Chief Flynn expected the captain and lieutenant themselves to address the problem through means consistent with the values of the MPD and constructive for the community.

Third, this captain and lieutenant looked outside their own organization to see if other police departments had confronted similar problems. In the search for alternative means of confronting the problem, Lieutenant Dubis identified and attended a professional conference that focused on people living on the street and highlighted several police responses to it. There she learned about an effort in another city that seemed relevant to Milwaukee.

Fourth, Dubis reached out to other agencies, thereby implicitly acknowledging that the MPD alone neither could nor should "own" the problem of street people. Solutions, or more accurately management, of the problems were to be found through police/social service agency collaboration.

Fifth, Dubis identified two highly motivated officers and provided them with special training. The trainers included representatives of other agencies, especially partnering organizations. This training was then extended to include additional officers, with plans to provide such training eventually to all patrol officers.

Finally, Dubis and the first two other officers participating in the effort were tasked with developing departmental guidelines for dealing with street people. These officers had gained an understanding of the problems of street people, expertise in the kinds of approaches police should take in dealing with them, and what other agencies were appropriate partners. This is a crucial step because police regularly use enormous discretion in deciding how to respond to particular events they encounter. While training of officers is a crucial first step in educating them about how to use discretion wisely, compassionately, and legally, guidelines help officers further. They make explicit the boundaries and goals that should shape officers' decisions: the principal values of the department; particular variables that should be considered (such as time, weather, offender and victim behavior, observers, and other such factors); and, finally, those elements that may not be considered (such as race or sexual orientation).

This is a classic example of community policing at work. Although routine, day-to-day operations of the MPD may not rise to the same level of carefully considered and crafted plans, the context for such efforts has been created by a vision of what policing is all about, the restructuring of the organization, changes in the administrative processes, and by the development of new relations with the public and private sectors.

Community-policing principles do not operate only in dealing with "soft" problems like homelessness; they operate in serious, violent crimes as well. In the two cases presented in Chapter Six—armed robberies from auto parts stores and city-wide armed robberies by "crews"—we see collaboration, decision making, and problem solving at the district level, the inclusion of special units (such as the TEU), detectives collecting and analyzing data along with crime analysts and sharing it with district officers, and the inclusion of outside agencies such as ATF. While both of these episodes represented acute criminal acts rather than chronic issues like homelessness, police applied a problem-solving approach: looking for patterns, applying analyses, examining records—all in stark contrast to the old police approach of responding to crimes only after they occurred.

LEADERSHIP AND THE MPD

The final question is whether or not the MPD has been restored to its position of leadership in American policing. The best answer that can be given at this time is that it depends. Certainly Milwaukee is once again hosting visitors from other police departments who are interested in what the MPD has accomplished and how it has done so. The list of is quite lengthy, and includes personnel from both the Detroit and New York City Police Departments. Flynn himself is one of the leading spokespersons for American policing in a group that includes New York City Police Commissioner William Bratton, Philadelphia's Commissioner "Chuck" Ramsey, and Los Angeles Police Chief "Charlie" Beck.

For all of these gains, however, much of Milwaukee's achievement and recognition will depend upon the extent to which the innovations of the last six years "stick"—that is, have they been implemented in such a way that they have captured the imagination of the city's leaders and the future leadership of the MPD, and will persist through subsequent administrations. Most likely compstat is in Milwaukee to stay; its demonstrated efficacy as both a crime analysis and planning guide and an interactive control system is too powerful to be set aside. (Even so, this does not mean that compstat meetings could not be trivialized in the future if they were conducted true to form but lacking in substance.) Perhaps detectives and their units might pose a threat. Detectives continue to have considerable status and political muscle. Michael Crivello, a detective who is president of the PPA (Milwaukee's police union), has been a constant critic of Flynn's reforms, especially as they impact detectives.[9] Politics too can play a part—say for example, a successful mayoral candidate who in exchange for union support agrees to appoint a future chief who will roll back important innovations.

Still, there are reasons to be optimistic. Police leadership in the United States has changed dramatically over the past decades. Most chiefs are well educated with at least a college degree. Many, like Flynn, have done graduate work or have law degrees. Leading chiefs have established working relationships with researchers who help departments develop police tactics through careful studies and who bring findings from other departments into the department's planning processes. Given the well-publicized success of many major American cities in crime prevention, chiefs who ignore or undo the methods that gave rise to these crime declines do so at great risk to their careers. Likewise, astute politicians will be careful about trying to roll back successful popular innovations. Citizens are coming to expect low crime rates: given an inquisitive press, the political need for continued crime declines (or maintenance of low levels of crime), and the public demand for order and safety, new chiefs may feel compelled to build upon the demonstrated successes of their predecessors. This does not mean that adjustments cannot or should not be made in virtually all or any elements of the MPD's strategy. It does mean that the current

9   Erik Gunn, "How Milwaukee Went Soft on Crime," *Politico Magazine*, November 11, 2014, http://www.politico.com/magazine/story/2014/11/milwaukee-soft-on-crime-112740.html?mi=m_t2_2h#.VGJ6p4ehbiZ.

vision of the MPD is persuasive, the basic outline of recent organizational and administrative changes are congruent with this vision, and the overall strategy is so coherent that moving in another direction may be inconceivable for the next several decades. The next chief will be important, but organizations make leaders as well as leaders make organizations.

INDEX